ON
NINETEEN EIGHTY-FOUR

ON
NINETEEN EIGHTY-FOUR

A BIOGRAPHY

D.J. Taylor

ABRAMS PRESS, NEW YORK

Library of Congress Control Number: 2018958830

ISBN: 978-1-4197-3800-5
eISBN: 978-1-68335-684-4

Printed and bound in the United States
10 9 8 7 6 5 4 3 2 1

ABRAMS The Art of Books
195 Broadway, New York, NY 10007
abramsbooks.com

For Peter Davison

That the year 1984 may come and go without the realization of the nightmare—with, indeed, an augmentation of personal freedom and a decay of corporate power—will not necessarily invalidate the horrible identification.

—ANTHONY BURGESS, writing in 1978

You must read it, sir. Then you will know why we must drop the atom bomb on the Bolshies!

—A New York newsvendor, placing a copy of *Nineteen Eighty-Four* into the hands of Isaac Deutscher, 1950s

CONTENTS

A NOTE ON MONETARY VALUES x

PART I   **Before (1903–1943)** xiii

1. THE TERRORS OF POWER 1
2. LIFE INTO ART 9
3. INFLUENCE AND INSPIRATION 28

PART II   **During (1943–1949)** 49

4. FITS AND STARTS 51
5. JURA DAYS 66
6. THE LAST MAN IN EUROPE 98

PART III   **After (1949 ad infinitum)** 115

7. COLD WAR WARRIORS 117
8. NEARING THE SELL-BY DATE 145
9. THE POST-TRUTH WORLD 158

Appendix: **The manuscript of
Nineteen Eighty-Four** 169

ACKNOWLEDGEMENTS 171
NOTES AND FURTHER READING 173
CHRONOLOGY 181
INDEX 189

A note on monetary values

For the majority of his professional career, Orwell was not at all well-paid. At certain points in the 1930s, his income dipped to as low as £250 a year ($1,250). The modern equivalent would be £16,000 to £17,000, or $21,000 to $22,000. In 1949, Orwell's advance against royalties for *Nineteen Eighty-Four* from his UK publisher was £300 ($1,200)—£10,000 to £11,000 ($13,000 to $14,500) today. For purposes of comparison, this was the annual salary of a middle-ranking London clerical worker.

George Orwell with his adopted son, Richard. Islington, London, 1946.

PART I
———

Before (1903–1943)

1. THE TERRORS OF POWER

IN THE EARLY SUMMER OF 1949, the first reviews of a new novel by an English writer named George Orwell began to appear in newspapers and magazines on either side of the Atlantic. If the initial batch of notices weren't universally ecstatic—several pundits were alarmed by the book's no-holds-barred torture scenes and its eerie, hallucinatory atmosphere—then no one was in any doubt that here was a work of the profoundest importance: not just a novel, the first band of readers insisted, but a terrifying vision of what the world might become if some of the political tendencies then animating its leaders were allowed to continue unchecked. The American critics were especially enthusiastic. 'This novel is the best antidote to the totalitarian disease that any writer has so far produced', Philip Rahv wrote in *Partisan Review*. 'Everyone should read it; and I recommend it particularly to those liberals who still cannot get over the political superstition that while absolute power is bad when exercised by the Right, it is in its very nature good, and a boon to humanity once the Left . . . take hold of it'. 'A brilliant and fascinating novel', Diana Trilling declared in *Nation*. British critics were no less vociferous. According to Harold Nicolson in the *Observer*, the author had set out 'to write a cautionary tale, by which to convince us of the terrible results which will follow if through inattention we allow our humanistic heritage to be submerged in a flood of materialism'.

Over in the *Times Literary Supplement*, Julian Symons thought that 'the picture of society in *Nineteen Eighty-Four* has an awful plausibility which is not present in other modern projections of our future' and praised a writer 'who is able to speak seriously and with originality of the nature of reality and the terrors of power'.

Terror. Fascination. Plausibility. Humanity's heritage in peril . . . As the summer went on, and copies of the book began to be distributed around continental Europe and in the debatable lands beyond it, these rivulets of approbation built into a tidal wave, the harbinger of an all-round media storm to which even Orwell—always downbeat about his chances of literary success—was not immune. 'The book seems to have had a good reception', he remarked to his agent, Leonard Moore, late in June, by which time 25,000 copies were available on the British market, 'i.e. even when unfavourable, I should say they are "selling" reviews'. Of the dozens of responses to *Nineteen Eighty-Four* filed in the first year of its existence—over sixty in the US alone—only a handful were unrepentantly hostile. One of them came from the American Communist journal *Masses & Mainstream*, whose reviewer, Samuel Sillen, complained of 'cynical rot', 'threadbare stuff with a tasteless sex angle', and lamented the 'ovation' the novel had received in the 'capitalist press'. Another could be found in *Pravda*, the official publication of the Soviet Communist Party, which condemned a work of 'misanthropic fantasy', a 'filthy book' redolent of the 'gruesome prognostications which are being made in our times by a whole army of venal writers on the orders and instigation of Wall Street'.

Pravda's reaction to what it assumed to be a capitalist plot is understandable, for *Nineteen Eighty-Four*—immediately banned in the Communist states of Eastern Europe and for decades available only in underground *samizdat* editions—is, transparently, an exposé of the totalitarian mind, the story of a man who rebels against the autocracy that is trampling on his soul. Here in the not-so-distant future, England has metamorphosed into 'Airstrip One', itself a part of 'Oceania', an agglomeration of territories ostensibly striving for precedence and military domination over the other great land blocs of 'Eurasia' and 'Eastasia'. It is a world of constant surveillance and devious propaganda, commanded by an organisation known as 'the Party', bossed by the all-seeing eye of 'Big Brother', and characterised by the brutal suppression of dissent ('thoughtcrime') and the routine falsification of the past. Winston Smith, its tormented late-thirtysomething hero, may only be a minor cog in this dictatorial wheel—a member of the 'Outer Party' with no privileges worth the name—but his part in the complex mechanisms of state control turns out to be a vital one. Sequestered in his cubicle at the fatally misnamed 'Ministry of Truth', Winston is charged with doctoring back-numbers of *The Times*, with a remit to airbrush out of history anyone deemed to have fallen foul of the regime's constantly changing official line. Ominously, the agent of this corruption is language itself, the savagely reductive code known as 'Newspeak', of which Winston's colleague, the soon-to-be-liquidated Syme, remarks, 'In the end we shall make thoughtcrime literally impossible, because there will be no words in which to express it'.

By the time this exchange takes place, Winston has embarked on his own particular thoughtcrime: the purchase of an antique, leather-bound book in which he begins to keep a diary; an affair with the much younger Julia, a fresh-faced but hard-bitten member of the puritanical 'Junior Anti-Sex League'; and late-night study of the legendarily proscribed volume written by the regime's great hate figure (plausibly to be identified with Trotsky) Emmanuel Goldstein, given to Julia by O'Brien, an apparently sympathetic member of the Inner Party. But O'Brien, alas, is merely an agent provocateur—Julia may even be acting as his willing accomplice—and Winston, dragged from the couple's refuge over an antique shop, is taken away to the Ministry of Love to be forcibly reintegrated into what passes as Oceanian society. It is at this point that the real implications of *Nineteen Eighty-Four*'s ideological armature are brought sharply into view. As a totalitarian regime constantly calls into question the historical justifications on which its power is based, turns one-time friends into enemies, and jettisons any position the moment it ceases to be useful, it follows that the concept of objective knowledge must be destroyed. Naturally, the means to destroy this knowledge is knowledge itself. Set against this yardstick, the tyrants of classical legend were merely opportunistic hooligans, altogether lacking the sophistication required to alter the shape of the past. The twentieth-century totalitarian, on the other hand—O'Brien's lectures on this subject are some of the most chilling passages in the book—is engaged on a far more sinister project: not to tell a man that $2 + 2 = 5$ and make him pretend to believe it, but to convince him that it is actually so. Tortured, browbeaten, and brainwashed, reduced to a snivelling pile of acquiescence, Winston wins the victory over himself. He loves Big Brother. The rebellion has failed.

The prodigious impact that *Nineteen Eighty-Four* had on its original audience was not simply a response to the horrors of Winston's degradation, his desperate exchanges with Julia ('Listen. The more men you've had, the more I love you. Do you understand that? . . . I hate virtue. I hate goodness. I don't want virtue to exist anywhere'), or the threatened unleashing of a cage-full of starving rats onto his unprotected face in the torture chamber of Room 101. Rather, it had to with their awareness that the dystopia Orwell had created was an artful projection of some of the geopolitical arrangements of the post-war world. As Orwell's first biographer, Bernard Crick, once remarked, '*Nineteen Eighty-Four* is misread if not read in the context of its time'. Here in 1949, a bare four years after the end of the Second World War, the context for Oceania's regime of authoritarian repression was that of the US–Soviet standoff which had followed Nazi Germany's surrender. Rather than capitalising on the Soviet Union's popularity on the world stage, and taking credit for the Red Army's titanic contribution to the war effort, Stalin had spent the period 1945–7 establishing a buffer along his western border and staffing the governments of newly liberated countries with his allies. There was stiff local opposition—the Communist Party managed only 17 per cent of the vote in Hungary's first (and only) free election of the post-war era—but by the end of 1945, Poland, Romania, and Bulgaria were all effectively satellite states.

If the first manoeuvrings of what came to be known as the 'Cold War' were calculated to alarm the US government, then the rhetoric that accompanied them—in particular Stalin's announcement early in 1946 that capitalism made war inevitable—only exacerbated the situation. It was like 'a delayed declaration of war against the United States' the US State Department anxiously proposed.

The idea that the world, or at any rate the western part of it, was ceasing to be a collection of independently minded sovereign states and turning into giant land masses whose future would depend on their military and technological might became a feature of the political discourse of the later 1940s. The multibillion-dollar Marshall Plan of 1947 was a deliberate attempt on the part of the US to support pro-American European states as they attempted to rebuild their shattered economies and protect their political systems from tyranny. 'I believe it must be the policy of the United States to support free peoples who are resisting subjugation by cruel minorities or by outside pressure', President Truman observed, as the rollout began. Simultaneously, the arms race begun by the detonation of the first two atomic bombs over Japan in August 1945 proceeded apace—between 1946 and 1948 the US exploded 23 separate devices on Bikini Atoll in the Marshall Islands—while the Soviets continued to tighten their grip on Eastern Europe. 'I went to Moscow as the foreign minister of an independent and sovereign state', a Czech politician complained, after a summons to the Kremlin in 1947. 'I returned as a Soviet slave'.

From the moment of its publication, *Nineteen Eighty-Four* could be regarded as the first Cold War novel. But to its British readers it had an even greater immediacy. Most previous dystopias—H.G. Wells's *When the Sleeper Wakes*, say, or Aldous Huxley's *Brave New World*—had been set on remote islands or in artificial never-never lands. Here the scenery is much more recognisable: post-war London cranked up a gear and put to sinister utilitarian purpose. It is not going too far to say that the appeal, and the resonance, of Winston's fictional struggle to its first audience, who wandered daily through a world of bomb craters and piled-up rubble, stemmed from the fact that it described and perverted a landscape they already knew. To particularise, any reader of *Nineteen Eighty-Four* who in 1949 headed west along the Strand—Orwell's bus route home from work during the period

1943–5, as it happens—would, having passed within earshot of the bells of St Clement Danes, the origin of the nursery rhyme 'Oranges and lemons, say the bells of St Clements', quoted at the moment when the Thought Police break in on Winston and Julia, very soon chance upon 'Victory Square' (Trafalgar Square). There he or she would find Nelson's Column, replaced in the novel by a statue of Big Brother celebrating his triumph in the Battle of Airstrip One. There, too, stood the church of St Martin-in-the-Fields, supposedly replaced by a propaganda museum full of waxwork tableaux. Other key landmarks were close by. Dominating Airstrip One's skyline, for example, is the Ministry of Truth ('an enormous structure of glittering white concrete'), clearly based on the University of London's Senate House and the wartime home of the Ministry of Information. All this topographical sleight of hand added up, and most post-war Londoners could be forgiven for finding the resemblances between Airstrip One and the world beyond their window a little too emphatic for comfort.

The sheer immediacy of *Nineteen Eighty-Four* was one of its strongest selling points. Here, unusually, was a novel that purported to be set in the future but appeared to borrow most of its scenery from the present: an alternative universe which, paradoxically, had its roots in the latest manifestations of post-war power politics. By the autumn of 1949, the book had turned into a runaway transatlantic success, been chosen by the US Book of the Month Club, synopsised by *Reader's Digest*—this guaranteed a six-figure sale—and eyed up by Broadway. It was all too late for Orwell; by the time the novel began its climb up the best-seller list, he was fatally ill with the tuberculosis that had been undermining his respiratory system for several years. Early negotiations with agent and publisher had been conducted from a sanatorium high up in the Gloucestershire hills. Then, towards the end of the summer, Orwell was removed by ambulance to University College London. There were faint hopes that he might rally—his friend Anthony Powell, who visited him in October, thought that in some respects 'he was in better form than I had ever seen him show'. Orwell himself acknowledged that a second marriage to a much younger woman named Sonia Brownell, conducted while he lay in his hospital bed by way of the Archbishop of Canterbury's special licence, had given him something to live for. But this was a false dawn. Another friend who saw him on Christmas afternoon reported that 'the stench of death was in the air, like autumn in a garden'. Occasionally, in these last days, he would reflect on the bitter irony of his success. 'I've made all this money', he told visitors, 'and now I'm going to die'. In the small hours of 21 January 1950, an artery burst in his lungs: he was dead within minutes.

He was much eulogised, and much mourned. Reading the obituaries on the day of his funeral, his friend Malcolm Muggeridge thought that he saw in them 'how the legend of a man is created'. The legend of *Nineteen Eighty-Four*—weaponised by the CIA, buttressed by a wall of film and TV adaptations, a potent source of inspiration to other creative artists, a staple of computer games and pop lyricists, quoted by politicians and read by millions of ordinary people—would continue to develop for the next seventy years, to the point where the book would come to be regarded as one of the key texts necessary for an understanding of the twenty-first century. Here in a world of demagogues, 'fake news', and ever more intrusive technology, Orwell can seem very much alive.

2. LIFE INTO ART

MOST ORWELL BIOGRAPHY IS, necessarily, an exercise in teleology: a journey through his life and times that starts with the achievement of *Nineteen Eighty-Four* and works backward in an attempt to establish exactly what it was about the years that preceded it that encouraged him to write the novel in the way that he did. What kind of person was he? Or, more important, what kind of person did he imagine himself to be? Nick Jenkins, the narrator of *A Dance to the Music of Time*, the twelve-volume *roman-fleuve* by Orwell's great friend Anthony Powell, once suggested that the crucial thing about the average human life is not what happens in it, but what the person experiencing it thinks happens in it—in other words, that the personal myths we construct around ourselves are just as, if not more, important than the verifiable facts of our existence. Any serious pursuit of Orwell has, consequently, to move on from the basic information of who he was and what he did to the much more enticing question of the kind of person he imagined himself to be.

Like many an early-twentieth-century Englishman, Orwell was a child of the Raj. He was born Eric Blair (a Christian name he always disliked) on 25 June 1903 in Motihari, Bengal, near the border with Nepal, where his father, Richard Walmesley Blair, worked for the Government of India's Opium Department, supervising the narcotics trade, which provided a large part of the administration's revenues. Blair senior, a twenty-year veteran of the British Empire's colonial service, was already in his mid-40s by the time his only son was born. When, in the year after his birth, Richard's wife, Ida Blair, took the infant Eric and his older sister, Marjorie, back to England, Richard naturally remained at his post. There was a brief period of leave in 1907, which produced a second daughter named Avril, but the result was that Orwell's childhood, mostly spent in Oxfordshire, was dominated by the figure of Ida Blair. Although Orwell loved his mother, and was loved by her in return, in later life he remembered his father only as a querulous, elderly man always saying 'don't'. The post of Sub-Deputy Opium Agent Fourth Class, to which Richard Blair eventually ascended, was a respectable job, but it was not well-paid, and the question of the family's social status hung like a pall over Orwell's childhood.

Or rather, Orwell tells us that it did. He was obsessed with class and some of his sharpest writing descends with a kind of homing instinct on the petty social distinctions that were so vital to the early-twentieth-century Englishman's sense of himself. There were distinguished ancestors—a distant relative had married the daughter of the Earl of Westmorland—family portraits, and antique silver winking from the cutlery drawer, but by the early 1900s the Blairs occupied a shabby-genteel niche in what the Earl's great-great-great-grandson defined, with characteristic precision, as 'the lower-upper-middle class'. The lack of money which Orwell diagnosed as the key theme of his upbringing meant that, as he once put it, his family's social expertise was always theoretical rather than actual. Theoretically, the Blairs were the kind of people who dressed for dinner, but in practice they could not afford sufficient servants to serve the kind of meal that people wearing dinner jackets and evening dresses would sit down to eat. Theoretically, their recreations included the traditional upper-class pursuits hunting, shooting, and fishing, but in practice they were never affluent enough to follow the hounds or slaughter pheasants.

The idea that, socially, the Blairs were there on sufferance followed Orwell into his adolescent life. He was a precociously clever boy, who won a scholarship to a fashionable preparatory school named St Cyprian's on the south coast of England (it was here that he met his lifelong friend the critic Cyril Connolly) and then, in the summer of 1917, with a second scholarship under his belt, proceeded amid clouds of academic glory to Eton College, near Windsor, the most prestigious of all the great English public schools. Many of the boys he met there would go on to pursue glittering careers, become politicians, diplomats, judges, or distinguished academics: the future British Prime Minister Lord Home was an exact contemporary. Orwell, on the other hand, did as little work as he could, scraped into the school's sixth form for a single term and exhibited all the classic signs of the disaffection that would colour his adult life: Connolly, who also went to Eton, characterised himself as a 'stage rebel'. Orwell, he insisted, was the real thing. There was no question of Orwell's following talented friends to Oxford and Cambridge. Instead, shortly after his eighteenth birthday, he opted to join another department of the British Empire's administrative outreach: the Burma Imperial Police.

The four and a half years that Orwell spent in the East are sometimes seen as a dreadful sentence of exile: a boy not yet out of his teens sent 8,000 miles to rot in possibly the least hospitable part of Britain's imperial fiefdom. In fact, for a young man of his age and social background who had failed to distinguish himself at school, it was a perfectly logical choice of career. The Blairs were old colonial hands; his mother's family, the Limouzins, were long established in the region; he had relatives living there. There is also a suggestion that, as a friend once put it, 'his imaginative powers, remarkable in one direction, did not run to a grasp of what any given job was really like'. At the same time, the Burma system was a tough one, with poorly trained assistant district commissioners despatched to stations in the wilds where only a solitary sergeant could speak English and the murder rate ran at 300 cases a year: the young men inducted into it grew up fast. The same confusion sometimes attends Orwell's return from the East in 1927. Orwell came back from Burma not to express his contempt for the Imperial project (although he was certainly disillusioned with it) but because he had fallen ill with dengue fever and been given six months' furlough. The decision to throw over his job, with the vague idea of 'becoming a writer', was taken sometime after the boat docked at Tilbury.

Already, some of the stanchions of *Nineteen Eighty-Four*, or at least some hints of the mental atmosphere it conjures up, are in place. By the age of 24, Orwell had spent several years working for what even pro-Imperialists acknowledged was an unusually repressive regime. In their more reflective moments, even the bores of the Kyauktada Club in *Burmese Days* (1934) seem aware of the Raj's stultifying effect on the indigenous Burmese. He had already—something that always needs to be taken into account when inspecting the novel's lurid, end-of-tether quality—begun to suffer from the ill health that was to dog his later life. Idealistic, determinedly old-fashioned in many of his cultural tastes, keen on 'books' but geographically, if not temperamentally, detached from the waves of modernist and experimental literature then breaking over the shores of Western Europe, he was also, friends imply, wary, superstitious, and, at times, convinced that he was being spied upon. A girl called Jacintha Buddicom, a romantic interest from his teenage years, remembered his being certain that the letters he sent home from Burma were being opened by the colonial authorities, and he once confided to his friend Richard Rees that seeing his name in print gave him an unpleasant feeling, 'for how can you be sure your enemy won't cut it out and work some sort of black magic on it?'

All this raises a line of enquiry that no attempt to discuss Orwell's literary career can altogether ignore: his outsider status. Most of the young men who arrived in the London literary world of the late 1920s and early 1930s got by on a series of personal connections that had either been forged at university or were a result of parental influence: Evelyn Waugh's first book, for example, was published by the firm of Duckworth, which employed his old Oxford friend Anthony Powell, and his second by Chapman & Hall, where his father was the managing director. If Orwell was not exactly friendless, then his years in Burma had cut him off from an important source of support and patronage. Compared to such up-and-coming contemporaries as Connolly (b. 1903), Powell (b. 1905), Waugh (b. 1903), and Graham Greene (b. 1904), he was starting from scratch, learning the rudiments of his craft while better-placed rivals were already seeing their first novels through the press. Progress was slow: it took five years for him to produce a publishable book (*Down and Out in Paris and London*, 1933), and at no time in the 1930s could he truthfully have described himself as a full-time writer. His base, for most of this long apprenticeship, was the Suffolk seaside town of Southwold, where the senior Blairs were spending their retirement. It was here that he returned in the intervals of amateur tramping that realised the English half of *Down and Out*, or came home in the holidays from a succession of private schools in which he taught. It was in Southwold, too, that he decided to adopt the alias of George Orwell: a good solid English name, he explained to his girlfriend Eleanor Jaques, derived from the King and the nearby river.

One makes this point to emphasize how comparatively unsuccessful Orwell was until at least his early 40s, how under-publicised and how comparatively under-rewarded. His only real hit before 1945's *Animal Farm* was *The Road to Wigan Pier* (1937), although very little of the money realised by the widely distributed Left Book Club edition went to the author himself. *Homage to Catalonia* (1938), a record of his experiences in the Spanish Civil War, sold only a few hundred copies: Fred Warburg, who published it, identified Orwell as 'a brilliant young author without a big success to his name'. His income in the later Thirties, when he and his first wife were managing—pretending to manage, some friends thought—a grocery shop in a tiny Hertfordshire village, seldom exceeded a few pounds a week, and his name was unknown beyond a small circle of readers: when his essay 'Boys' Weeklies' appeared in Connolly's monthly magazine *Horizon* in the early part of 1940, Connolly received an enthusiastic letter from his proprietor, Peter Watson, asking who George Orwell was. As late as 1946, at work on a first draft of *Nineteen Eighty-Four*, he could be found diffidently informing his literary executor, 'If I should peg out in the next few years, I don't really think there'll be a great deal for you to do except deal with publishers over reprints and decide whether or not to keep a few miscellaneous documents'.

The idea that whatever he did he would not succeed is central to the view that Orwell took of himself. It is not going too far to say that for most of his adult life, he was obsessed with the idea of failure. Life, he once wrote, was a succession of defeats, and only the very young or the very foolish believed otherwise. As for the baggage from that life that he carried on into the world of his final novel, *Nineteen Eighty-Four* is full of tiny fragments of detail, hoarded over the decades, some of them clearly borrowed from Orwell's childhood in the Oxfordshire back lanes. Anthony Burgess has pointed out quite how *rural* much of the novel's figurative language becomes—O'Brien talking of taking a child from its mother as one takes an egg from a hen; the three contending super-states spoken of as leaning on each other to keep themselves upright 'like three stooks in a hayfield'. Or there is the moment at which Winston notes that his glass of stinking 'Victory Gin' gives off 'a sickly oily smell, as of Chinese rice-spirit', which is not a comparison that the London-bound Winston Smith could have made, but Orwell the one-time Burma policeman remembering his years in the East.

Sometimes the baggage is more lavishly unpacked. One might note the scene in which Winston, dragged from his hidey-hole above Mr Charrington's antique shop by the Thought Police, is taken off to be interrogated at the Ministry of Love. Here several different echoes from Orwell's early life clamour to be heard. To begin with, there is the episode's strong resemblance to an unpublished sketch entitled 'Clink', written as far back as August 1932. This describes an incident in which Orwell, hot in pursuit of journalistic 'copy', drank himself into insensibility in a north London pub and then staggered out into the street with the deliberate aim of getting himself arrested. The stratagem worked and he was detained for forty-eight hours at Bethnal Green police station in the East End, charged with being incapably drunk and fined 6 shillings. The sketch may be straightforward reportage—no one is about to be beaten up by the Thought Police or taken off to be tortured—but the situational background, as described by Orwell in 1932, is strikingly similar: 'They kept us waiting for several hours. It was beastly uncomfortable in the cell, for there was not room for all of us to sit down on the plank bed, and it was beastly cold in spite of the number of us'.

So, too, is the grim relish of physical detail. Like the Ministry of Love, the police cell lacks adequate sanitation ('Several men used the W.C., which was disgusting in so small a space, especially as the plug did not work . . . the nasty faecal stench in the cell became unbearable'). But by far the sharpest twitch on the thread comes at the moment when, sitting waiting for the summons to 'Room 101', Winston is joined by a 'mean-looking man who might have been an engineer or a technician of some kind'. Skull-faced and with bulging eyes, the man is clearly starving. Recognising his distress, one of the other prisoners reaches into the pockets of his overalls and brings out a piece of bread. There is a furious roar from the telescreen and a disembodied voice yells, 'Bumstead! 2713 Bumstead J! Let fall that piece of bread'. Who is Bumstead J? This turns out to be a reference to a man named Jack Bumstead, the son of a Southwold grocer with whom the Blairs had dealt in the 1930s, reinvented and put to work in a novel set in an imaginary future at least a decade after Orwell had last set eyes on him.

And then there is *Nineteen Eighty-Four*'s great climactic horror—what lurks, starving and vengeful, inside the cage in Room 101. Orwell's rat obsession is a fixture of his printed work, so much so that he can often seem like a kind of literary pied piper dancing at the head of an unappeasable furry brood that winds on from one book to the next. From the memory of the specimens he had shot as a teenager by the light of an acetylene bicycle lamp to the testimony of a 'vermin man', met in the course of one of his tramping excursions, who told him that it was not safe to enter the kitchens of certain London restaurants without a loaded revolver, rats are everywhere in Orwell: the two outsize creatures he had once seen on a kitchen table in Paris gnawing at a ham that had been left out there the night before; the 'great bloated brutes' seen scampering through the trenches in Spain, 'too impudent even to run away unless you shot at them', or splashing along a ditch and 'making as much noise as if they were otters'. Even in *Down and Out in Paris and London*, entering a cheap lodging house in the East End for the first time, he notes that 'it seemed to me like going down into some dreadful subterranean place—a sewer full of rats, for instance'. If there was one thing he hated, Orwell once remarked, it was a rat running over him in the dark. The rat phobia burns on into *Nineteen Eighty-Four*. Of all the novel's terrors, the scene in which Winston, hauled into Room 101 and confronted with the thing he most fears, glimpses the grey muzzles and the yellowing teeth has the greatest impact: not only for the horror it inspires, but also for the reader's growing suspicion that it taps into an anxiety that is central to Orwell's life.

BETWEEN 1934 AND 1939, Orwell published four full-length novels. A few stylistic flourishes and avant-garde abstractions aside, they are works of scrupulous realism set in locales that would have been instantly recognisable to the comparatively few people who bought and read them. Each, though, turns out to be quietly prefigurative of the nightmare landscapes of *Nineteen Eighty-Four*. Flory in *Burmese Days* (1934) is a disaffected colonial timber merchant with a weakness for the whisky bottle and a native mistress, convinced that he can redeem the sterility of his life by marrying a newcomer to the remote provincial township where he frets out his leisure hours. *A Clergyman's Daughter* (1935) features a neurotic spinster named Dorothy Hare, who, after mysteriously losing her memory, finds herself tramping the streets of London, picking hops in Kent, and finally teaching in a down-at-heel private school. Gordon Comstock, the hero of *Keep the Aspidistra Flying* (1936), alternatively, is a moth-eaten poet who agonises over his rejection slips and, desperate to preserve his integrity from the assaults of the 'money God', throws over a safe job in advertising to work in a bookshop. In *Coming Up for Air* (1939), plump, middle-aged George Bowling, trapped in a stultifying marriage to the mirthless Hilda, sets off on an illicit trip to rediscover the world of his Oxfordshire boyhood.

As for what links Flory, Hare, Comstock, and Bowling to Winston Smith's journeys through the bombed-out streets of Airstrip One, one of the key preoccupations of Orwell's early work is the idea of manipulation, represented by the malign exterior forces that can be seen interfering in his characters' lives. If the people in his early novels share an abiding characteristic, it is Orwell's tendency to isolate and victimise them, to place them, alone or relatively friendless, at the centre of a hostile world from which they cannot escape and where their every movement is subject to constant surveillance. 'Knype Hill', a very thinly disguised Southwold, in *A Clergyman's Daughter* is portrayed as a kind of ant heap of malicious gossip and carefully nursed grudges, where spite conquers Christian charity and everybody is always eavesdropping on their neighbours' conversation and scheming to do them down. 'It was one of those sleepy, old-fashioned streets, that look so ideally peaceful on a casual visit and so very different when you live in them and have an enemy or a creditor behind every window', Orwell remarks of the town's principal thoroughfare. *Burmese Days*, set mostly in Kyauktada's Kipling-haunted European Club, strikes exactly the same note, or rather goes a step beyond it to characterise colonial Burma as essentially a totalitarian society. 'It is a stifling, stultifying world in which to live', Flory tells his Indian friend Dr Veraswami. 'It is a world in which every word and every thought is censored . . . Free speech is unthinkable'.

All Orwell's principal characters, it soon emerges, are victims of the same authorial sleight of hand: detached, deracinated, exposed, forever at the mercy of vast, unappeasable forces it is futile to resist. Gordon Comstock may only have to contend with his vigilant landlady, Mrs Wisbeach, but even so the life he spends in a rented room in seedy north-west London is an endless series of concealments: brewing illicit cups of tea while listening to the sound of feet on the stair or surreptitiously flushing parcels of used tea leaves down the lavatory pan. George Bowling, too, has a terror of being found out. His mournful, elegiac journey around the Thames Valley haunts of his boyhood may be entirely innocent, but he is transfixed by the thought that, against all the odds, his wife's emissaries will be on his tail, and when he half-hears an emergency radio broadcast in which a woman with his wife's name is said to be dangerously ill, it seems obvious to him that this is one of Hilda's 'dodges', a devious practical joke dreamed up with the deliberate aim of making him suffer. If Orwell had yet to come up with the idea of the telescreen, *Nineteen Eighty-Four's* great symbolic invention and the one that moves it closest to some of the technological refinements of the twenty-first century, then the idea that we live in a world where our autonomy will always be constrained by an eavesdropping authority was already at the forefront of his mind.

But the strongest connection between Orwell's Thirties quartet and Winston Smith is what ultimately happens to them. Each rebels against the agencies that are out to bring them down, and each is eventually forced to retreat, capitulate, or at any rate reach some accommodation with the forces that, either directly or indirectly, control their lives. Flory, who makes the mistake of offending a powerful native magistrate, is thrown over by the alluring Elizabeth and shoots himself. After her adventures among the tramps and in Mrs Creevy's down-at-heel private school, Dorothy ends up back in her father's rectory, re-entombed in a grisly existence of alarm clocks summoning her to attend Holy Communion and late-night sessions spent manufacturing costumes for the church pageant over the glue pot's penetrating reek. Gordon emerges from the Lambeth slum in which he has fetched up to marry his pregnant girlfriend, inhabit a furnished flat in the Edgware Road, and return to the sedative embrace of a 'proper job'. Disillusioned by his re-encounter with Lower Binfield, where the pool full of giant fish that stalked his imagination has been converted into a rubbish dump, Bowling hastens meekly back to suburbia to face Hilda's wrath. Like Winston, each of them has won a victory over themselves, and the destinies they struggled to avoid are, in the end, inescapable. The best they can hope for is a kind of coming to terms with this slow process of mental subjugation, a minute adjustment to occupation or worldview that has the effect of reminding them who they really are.

But there is something else going on amid these stories of stasis, rebellion, and defeat. It is not only that Flory, Dorothy Hare, Comstock, and Bowling are cut from the same cloth as the Ministry of Truth's reality tamperer. At the same time, the imaginative world in which their journeys are framed harbours a series of prophetic notes, devious foreshadowings of the territory subsequently staked out by *Nineteen Eighty-Four*. *A Clergyman's Daughter* opens with Dorothy being dragged awake by the noise of the alarm clock—'a horrid little bomb of bell metal'. The aeroplanes are coming, Gordon reflects, early on in *Keep the Aspidistra Flying*; soon the whole world will be going up in a roar of high explosive. His very surname turns out to prefigure one of the truncations of Newspeak ('Comstock' = 'Common Stock'). 'My poems are dead because I'm dead. You're dead. We're all dead people in a dead world', he lectures his girlfriend Rosemary, just as, over a decade later—emerging from a meditation in which he decides that 'the only victory lay in the far future, long after you were dead, that from the moment of declaring war on the Party it was better to think of yourself as a corpse'—Winston will starkly inform Julia that 'We are the dead'. The streets that Winston surveys from his eyrie in Victory Mansions, where 'little eddies of wind were whirling dust and torn paper into spirals', offer the same view as the vista that adjoins Gordon's Hampstead bookshop where 'a ribbon of paper fluttered like a tiny pennant'. And then there is the advertising campaign that Gordon works on after his return to the agency, a remedy for sweaty feet rammed home by the slogan '"P.P." [pedic perspiration])—WHAT ABOUT YOU?' If this is thought to possess a 'sinister simplicity', then it also seems only a step or two away from the looming terrors of Big Brother and the Thought Police.

These twitches on the thread are never more insistent than in Orwell's sorrowings over the 'golden country'—the idea of a rural idyll to which the hero can escape, usually accompanied by a woman, and forget the cares that assail him for an hour or two. Old friends noted his tendency to let himself go when he attempted to link his love of nature with his love of women. In *Nineteen Eighty-Four*, this finds expression in a passage in Chapter 3 in which Winston lies dreaming of his early life and the tragedy of his mother's death.

> Suddenly he was standing on short springy turf, on a summer evening when the slanting rays of the sun gilded the ground. The landscape that he was looking at recurred so often in his dreams that he was never fully certain whether or not he had seen it in the real world. In his waking thoughts he called it the Golden Country. It was an old, rabbit-bitten pasture, with a foot-track wandering across it and a molehill here and there. In the ragged hedge on the opposite side of the field the boughs of the elm trees were swaying very faintly in the breeze, their leaves just stirring in dense masses like women's hair. Somewhere near at hand, though out of sight, there was a clear, slow-moving stream where dace were swimming in the pools under the willow trees.

Summer pasture and 'gilded' ground; the thought of rabbits, moles, and dace swimming in their pools; leaves stirring like women's hair. It is an intensely realised passage, born out of a deep longing for the reflective, slow-moving rural life that Orwell had relished as a child, and paragraphs like it lie strewn all over his early work. In *Burmese Days*, Flory and Elizabeth amble side by side across a stubble field: 'The sun was going down beyond the Irrawaddy. The light shone yellow across the field, gilding the stubble stalks and striking into their faces with a yellow, gentle beam'. There are the same atmospherics—the declining sun, the springy ground—and, significantly, even some of the same figurative effects. A very similar scene occurs in *Keep the Aspidistra Flying* where Gordon and Rosemary make a weekend trip to Burnham Beeches, twenty miles outside London, where once again the sunshine floods the fields and the glimpse of a rabbit leaping up from its burrow sends them into raptures. Bowling, meanwhile, is the Golden Country's very own resident game warden, a 45-year-old insurance salesman fixated, like his creator, on the world of his Edwardian childhood, forever dreaming of the long, rambling walks he took through the Oxfordshire verdure and the pools of giant carp just waiting for some intrepid fisherman to lay them waste.

If all Orwell's pre-1939 characters are in some sense 'coming up for air', surfacing for a brief gasp of freedom before the water closes once more over their heads, then the account of George Bowling's attempt to rediscover some of the territory of his lost past is *Nineteen Eighty-Four*'s most obvious dry run. A veteran of the conflict of 1914–18, monitoring the news from continental Europe with an increasingly anxious glance, Bowling is less agitated by the prospect of a Second World War ('It's coming soon, that's certain') than by the future that stretches out beyond it.

> But it isn't the war that matters, it's the after-war. The world we're going down into, the kind of hate-world, slogan-world. The coloured shirts, the barbed wire, the rubber truncheons. The secret cells where the electric light burns night and day, and the detectives watching you while you sleep. And the processions and the posters with enormous faces, and the crowds of a million people all cheering for the Leader until they deafen themselves into thinking that they really worship him, and all the time, underneath, they hate him so that they want to puke. It's all going to happen.

Written late in 1938 or early in 1939, this is, on the most basic level, a response to the newsreel pictures of Hitler and Stalin, but is also uncannily prefigurative of the world of Big Brother, Two Minutes Hate, and the torture chambers of the Ministry of Love, Orwell busily extrapolating the landscapes of interwar-era England into a future that he fears Hitler and Stalin will have helped to create. *Coming Up for Air* extends to more than one revelation of this kind, all the more pointed in that they tend to be framed in the context of Bowling's nostalgia. Quite early on in the novel, he stops an elegiac recitation of the principal British coarse fish ('Roach, rudd, dace, bleak, barbel . . .') to reflect these are 'solid kind of names. The people who made them up hadn't heard of machine guns, they didn't live in terror of the sack or spend their time eating aspirins, going to the pictures, and wondering how to keep out of the concentration camp'.

The reflections about 'the after-war' steal into Bowling's head as he sits at a meeting of the West Bletchley Left Book Club listening to a lecture on 'The Menace of Fascism'. Even more significant, perhaps, is his decision to pay a late-night visit to his friend Porteous once the meeting has ended. In the context of *Coming Up for Air*'s conspicuous realism, Porteous, a retired public school Classics master, who lives a monastic life in rented lodgings, regards the contemporary world with a glacial detachment, and complains about the noise of his upstairs neighbour's radio, is something of an anomaly. You suspect that, in the end, he is not the kind of acquaintance that Bowling could have made in the course of his insurance-peddling, pub-haunting daily existence, but there to make a point, play devil's advocate in an argument begun simply to allow his visitor to express what he most deeply feels about the way the twentieth-century world is changing. Admitted to Porteous's digs, waved into an armchair, and supplied with a whisky and soda, Bowling is ready to be soothed by his host's talk of the classical world, only to discover that he cannot get the lecturer's voice out of his head. Finally, he interrupts Porteous to ask: What does he think of Hitler?

Predictably, the retired schoolmaster thinks nothing of the Nazi leader ('I see no reason for paying any attention to him . . . These people come and go. Ephemeral, purely ephemeral'.) But Bowling isn't so sure. As he explains:

> I think you've got it wrong. Old Hitler's something dif-
> ferent. So's Joe Stalin. They aren't like these chaps in
> the old days who crucified people and chopped their
> heads off and so forth, just for the fun of it. They're

after something new—something that's never been heard of before.

This, too, points the reader firmly in the direction of *Nineteen Eighty-Four*'s ideological core. The new breed of tyrant, Bowling insists, is not interested in power as a way of achieving things but as an end in itself. By extension, a totalitarian regime will always plot to deny its subjects freedom not because it will make them better citizens, or help the state to achieve its military or political ends, but because this is what a totalitarian regime does.

The argument winds on desultorily for an hour or so—Porteous, naturally, is unconvinced by the idea of Hitler's novelty—buttressed by talk of 'the eternal verities', but there is an odd moment, towards its end, when Bowling, looking at the older man as he leans against the bookshelf reading aloud from a volume of poetry, is struck by the sensation that his host is dead. Not literally so, but ghostlike—sentient, knowledgeable, and amusing, but with a brain that has effectively ceased to function. Like many decent people, Bowling reflects, his mind has stopped. 'They can't defend themselves against what's coming to them, because they can't see it, even when it's under their noses. They think that England will never change and that England's the whole world. Can't grasp that it's a leftover, a tiny corner that the bombs happen to have missed'. That the bombs won't, in the end, leave England unscathed is suggested by a scene during Bowling's return to Lower Binfield when a passing RAF plane accidentally drops its load on the High Street. In among the smashed crockery of a devastated greengrocer's shop 'there was lying a leg. Just a leg, with the trouser still on it and a black boot with a Wood-Milne rubber heel'. In exactly the same way, Winston Smith clambers to his feet in the aftermath of a 'steamer' rocket raid on Airstrip One to discover that the object left lying in the road in its wake is a severed human hand.

Coming Up for Air was written shortly before the events of summer 1939, when the outbreak of war followed hard on the heels of the announcement of a Nazi-Soviet pact. Despite their formal ideological separations, Fascism and Communism could now be regarded as essentially versions of the same thing, a point that the novel is keen to emphasize. 'Gang up, choose your leader', Bowling gloomily reflects as he watches the Left Book Club's lecturer in action. 'Hitler's black and Stalin's white. But it might just as well be the other way about, because in the little chap's mind both Hitler and Stalin are the same. Both mean spanners and smashed faces'. Here in the last summer before the war, almost a decade before *Nineteen Eighty-Four* made its presence felt on the bookshop shelves, Orwell was already worming his way deep into the heart of the totalitarian mind.

3. INFLUENCE AND INSPIRATION

HANGING OVER NEARLY ALL of Orwell's pre-1939 life is the question of how he came by the political beliefs that allowed him to claim that Hitler and Stalin were 'after something new—something that's never been heard of before'. After all, the returning Burma policeman who sat down in his parents' house in Southwold in the late 1920s with the aim of becoming a writer had had some very different ends in view. 'Why I Write', a literary *apologia pro vita sua*, written in 1946, contains a fascinating statement of what Orwell thought his ambitions were as a very young man:

> So it is clear what kind of books I wanted to write in so far as I could be said to want to write books at that time. I wanted to write enormous naturalistic novels with unhappy endings, full of detailed descriptions and arresting similes, and also full of purple passages in which words were used partly for the sake of their sound.

And, as he straightaway goes on to acknowledge, *Burmese Days* ('which I wrote when I was thirty but projected much earlier') is exactly this kind of book, a novel whose real subject, as he later admitted, was the local landscape, where light rains down like 'glistening white oil', campfire flames dance 'like red holly', and canoes move through the water 'like long curved needles threading through embroidery'. It is not that the novel lacks a political focus—the people wandering around in it are clearly either the beneficiaries or the victims of a repressive regime, and one only has to attend to a paragraph or two of Flory's bitter exchanges with the meek-mannered (and unashamedly pro-British) Dr Veraswami to comprehend his true feelings about the ideology it serves. Rather, it is that the lurking spectre of the Raj, with its scarred-buttock prisoners and hanging details, is only a single element in Flory's sense of his own victimhood and his sequestration in an alien land. In some ways the purple birthmark that disfigures his face and his lack of money are quite as much a part of his disaffection as the colonial system which his work upholds, and when the aristocratic army officer Lieutenant Verrall threatens to displace him in Elizabeth's affections it is significant that his immediate response is straightforward envy. With his sinewy frame, his fearlessness, and his complete disregard for what other people think of him, Verrall is clearly someone that Flory would very much like to be.

The same sense of a personal dilemma silently displacing any kind of ideological focus rises from the two novels that followed. If *A Clergyman's Daughter* is essentially a matter of Orwell stitching together materials from his own life—the time spent in Southwold, the hop-picking excursion to Kent, the teaching days in West London—into a none-too-convincing whole, then it is not in any obvious sense a political book: the only forces actively oppressing Dorothy Hare are her tyrannical father, the gossips of the Knype Hill tearooms, and the warped sensibility that these afflictions have conjured up in her mind. Unlike Dorothy, Gordon

Comstock in *Keep the Aspidistra Flying* has specific targets in his sights—he hates the 'Money God', inveighs against the capitalist racket, and despises the industry that employs him as 'the last rattling of the swill bucket'—but there is little sense of solidarity in his response and his conversations with Ravelston, the friendly left-leaning magazine editor, are always aimed at exposing some of the flaws in Marxist theory rather than to burnish it up. In the end, when the smoke rises from the emotional battlefield on which these complaints are made, all that is left is an angry and embittered young man who is furious that literary editors won't publish his poems and that his girlfriend won't sleep with him. Gordon's real enemy, you sometimes feel, is the fate that dealt him what he presumes to be a bad hand in life.

And if Orwell's early novels are less interested in politics than in dramatizing some of his beliefs about human behaviour, then neither do his unpublished writings of the period have much to say about his political beliefs. In the context of interwar-era British life, this lack of interest in the world beyond the window is rather startling. The early 1930s, the years of Ramsay Mac-Donald's National Government and three million unemployed, were a volatile period in British politics, full of mounting unease, disquieting news from central Europe, and an overwhelming conviction that the old certainties of the pre–Great War period had been blown into fragments. To most British people the country's decision to go off the Gold Standard in the autumn of 1931 was a symbol of waning power and international prestige. The activities of right-wing extremists, such as the Fascist 'Blackshirts' led by the former Labour MP Sir Oswald Mosley, were widely reported in the press. Orwell's view of the political and economic ferment going on around him can seem curiously detached. Take, for example, his attitude to the great financial crisis of autumn 1931, which culminated, six weeks later, with the re-election of MacDonald's coalition with a majority of over 500 seats. Quite by chance, Orwell occupied a ringside seat on these proceedings. At this point he was living in a hostel in Tooley Street, London SE1, and making early-morning trips to the fish market in nearby Billingsgate in search of casual work. The Bank of England's headquarters in Threadneedle Street were only a short distance away, but Orwell's diaries and letters make no mention of the daily news bulletins issuing from its press office other than to remark to his friend Eleanor that 'I don't understand or take any interest in politics'.

Much of this incomprehension can be detected in what is often assumed to be his first serious engagement with practical politics—the trip he took to the economically blighted north of England in the early part of 1936 that gave rise to *The Road to Wigan Pier* (1937). It is tempting to regard this mixture of reportage and polemic, published in the orange covers of Victor Gollancz's recently established Left Book Club, as a mark of newfound political awareness—a writer determined to bring back news from the distressed areas with the aim of advertising a set of recently acquired beliefs for a sponsor who made no secret of his political stance: Gollancz, whose yellow-jacketed titles were one of the great publishing success stories of the 1930s, employed several members of staff with links to the Communist Party of Britain's headquarters in King Street, London. In fact, Orwell's journey north in January 1936 seems to have been undertaken for much more humdrum reasons. As he explained in a letter to a friend, 'Now that my book [*Keep the Aspidistra Flying*] is done I am giving up my job at the bookshop, as it is hardly worth going on working for £1 a week, which is all I am getting now, and as soon as I can arrange it I am going up to the north of England to try and get material for some kind of book about the industrial districts'. As for why a hard-up journalist in search of copy might want to make his way around the backstreets of Liverpool, Leeds, and Sheffield, this, it should be pointed out, was the great age of the English travelogue—often, but not always, conceived with the aim of reporting on social conditions. J.B. Priestley's genre-defining *English Journey* had appeared in 1934. At precisely the same moment that Orwell set out from London, Aldous Huxley was making plans to visit the Nottinghamshire coalfields. None of this is to impugn Orwell's motives, or mark him down as an opportunist or a poverty tourist, but there is a sketchiness about the original impetus that took him north ('some kind of book') that seems to call its ideological basis into question.

The same is true of the journey itself, where Orwell often seems to cast himself in the role of an anthropologist venturing into unfamiliar territory rather than someone keen on having his beliefs corroborated or his assumptions incrementally refined. When he describes someone met along the way as 'taking a prominent part in the Socialist Movement', you suspect that he knew very little about socialist movements or what taking a prominent part in them implied. As Robert Colls points out in his excellent book about Orwell and Englishness, at this stage in his political development he knew no Labour Party history, seemed to regard socialism as some kind of fad, and took no interest in any of the institutions trying to make life better for the people he had come to observe. Even when the trip was finished he seems to have been uncertain what to do with the material he had accumulated—a letter to Richard Rees notes that 'I haven't made up my mind yet'—and as late as October 1936, six months after his return, Victor Gollancz could be found writing to inquire of Orwell's agent just exactly what his client was up to. Selection for the Left Book Club, with its guarantee of high sales, came late on in the proceedings, which rather serves to emphasize the piecemeal, provisional quality that hangs over the project.

It is tempting to regard 1936 as the decisive year in Orwell's existence: the year when he first began to take a serious interest in politics; the year in which he began to move beyond the self-projecting world of his first three novels; and the year in which he finally found some kind of emotional security. In April, back from northern England, and quartered in the Hertfordshire village of Wallington, he married a girl named Eileen O'Shaughnessy, two years younger than him, whom he first met during his bookselling days in Hampstead. From the angle of the male-dominated 1930s, Eileen was a comparatively unusual specimen: an educated woman, who had studied English Literature at Oxford and then taken a master's degree at University College London. Although devoted to her husband, she had no illusions about the things that most concerned him. Talking once about her much-loved brother Laurence, who she believed would come to her aid at a moment's notice from the other side of the world, she observed that 'George would not do that. For him, work comes before anything'. Nonetheless, friends noted the positive effect she had on Orwell, cheering him up, taking him out of himself, and organising his domestic life. It was a 'proper marriage', Orwell once reflected, characterised by give-and-take and shared intellectual interests. Clever, good-humoured, and well-read, Eileen had a profound influence on the alternative worlds that Orwell came to create, and her involvement is no less substantial for being indirect.

IF THERE IS ANY HINT of the landscapes of Oceania in *The Road to Wigan Pier* it comes in some of the domestic detail of working-class English life. There is, for example, a passage in *Nineteen Eighty-Four* in which Winston broods about 'decaying, dingy cities where underfed people shuffled to and fro in leaky shoes, in patched-up nineteenth-century houses that smelt always of cabbage and bad lavatories', only to find the train of thought leading towards his put-upon neighbour and her plumbing problems. 'He seemed to see a vision of London, vast and ruinous, city of a million dustbins, and mixed up with it was a vision of Mrs Parsons, a woman with lined face and wispy hair, fiddling helplessly with a blocked waste-pipe'. One or two other visions of urban decay had followed him home from the north, and Mrs Parsons's tribulations echo a famous passage in which, passing through the outskirts of Wigan by train, Orwell catches sight of a young woman at the back of a slum house pushing a stick up the lead waste pipe. 'She looked up as the train passed, and I was almost near enough to catch her eye. She had a round, pale face, the usual exhausted face of the slum girl who is twenty-five and looks forty . . . and it wore, for the second in which I saw it, the most desolate, hopeless expression I have ever seen'.

By the time these words appeared in print, Orwell was already immersed in what would prove to be the defining political event of his life. This was the Spanish Civil War, in which he spent six months fighting on the Republican side, was shot through the throat by a sniper (the bullet missed his carotid artery by a few millimetres), and came face to face with one or two of the consequences of dissension in a conflict where a single dominating ideology held sway. As with *The Road to Wigan Pier*, Orwell was cagey about the impulse that sent him to Spain. He left England in the last week of 1936, he told readers of *Homage to Catalonia* (1938), with the vague aim of writing some newspaper articles. This, though, is to downplay the evidence of the people to whom he bade his farewells: the magazine editor to whom he confided that 'something must be done', the friend to whom he patiently explained that if everyone who went to Spain killed a Fascist there wouldn't be many of them left, or the publisher who met him shortly before he left and recalled him saying 'I want to go to Spain and have a look at the fighting . . . Good chaps the Spaniards, can't let them down'. It is also to understate the revelatory excitement of some of the letters he sent home (he had seen 'great things', he told Connolly) or the way in which his mind continued to dwell on his experiences long after the conflict had ended. Even on his death bed, Malcolm Muggeridge remembered, he was still talking about the war and the part he had played in it.

Why was Spain so important to Orwell? One clue lies in his account of the situation in Barcelona when he arrived there in the early days of 1937. Here, he decided, was a city which, almost overnight, had achieved genuine social equality, where the middle classes were lying low and the power of the Catholic Church seemed to have vanished, where the bootblacks addressed their clients as *Usted* ('You') rather than *Señor* ('Sir'), and he was once reprimanded by a hotel manager for trying to tip the lift boy. 'How easy it is to make friends in Spain', he wistfully remembered. A poem he wrote some years later, recalling the Italian militiaman who had greeted him on his arrival at the Lenin Barracks, marshals all the emotions Spain inspired in him—generosity, fellow-feeling, a cause being more important than nationhood or class—in a single stanza:

> But the thing that I saw in your face
> No power can disinherit
> No bomb that ever burst
> Shatters the crystal spirit.

But another clue lies in the political background to Orwell's months in Spain. Essentially the Spanish Civil War operated on two interconnected levels. If, on one level, it was an internal conflict between a democratically elected Republican government and a Nationalist Falange, then, at the same time, it was a proxy war conducted beneath the gaze of international superpowers each keen to ensure that their own side came out on top. Orwell's first plan had been to make his way there under the auspices of the pro-Soviet British Communist Party. But the interview with the party's general secretary Harry Pollitt had not gone well, and the letter of introduction he eventually took with him was addressed to the Barcelona representative of the Independent Labour Party (ILP). In strict political terms, this meant that Orwell's card was already marked. Although the struggle against Franco's Nationalist forces was officially being waged by a 'Popular Front' that supposedly united all the parties of the Spanish left, the reality was sharply different. In Barcelona, where Orwell informed the ILP representative of his intention to join one of the Republican militias, much of the running was being made by anarchist-leaning organisations such as the National

Confederation of Labour (CNT) and the United Workers Marxist Party (POUM). In volunteering for the POUM, prior to his departure for the Huesca Front, Orwell immediately made himself an object of suspicion to the orthodox left, as represented by the International Marxist Brigade, and the large number of Soviet agents flooding into the country.

Few of these internal tensions were evident to Orwell when he arrived at the Lenin Barracks in January 1937. As he acknowledges in *Homage to Catalonia*:

> When I came to Spain and for some time afterwards, I was not only uninterested in the political situation but unaware of it. I knew there was a war on, but I had no notion of what kind of a war. If you had asked me why I had joined the militia I should have answered 'To fight against Fascism', and if you had asked me what I was fighting *for*, I should have answered 'Common decency'.

But by the time he left Spain six months later, left-wing faction fights were an inextricable part of the legacy he took with him. When he came back to Barcelona in the spring it was to find that the factional disputes had spilled over into street fighting between the Civil Guard and the CNT; he and his militia comrades spent three days on the rooftop of a cinema scanning the thoroughfares for signs of trouble. Subsequently members of the POUM were declared to be covert Fascists. Orwell's ability to monitor the rise of Soviet influence in Barcelona was interrupted by his despatch to the Aragon Front, and the early-morning encounter with the sniper's bullet: returning to Barcelona for the final time in early summer, and reunited with Eileen, he discovered that many of his

comrades—including his company commander Georges Kopp—
were in jail and that a warrant had been issued for his and Eileen's
arrest. After several days spent dodging the authorities, and in
Orwell's case sleeping in derelict buildings, they managed to cross
the French border by train.

Several other writers who had travelled to Spain in 1937
underwent similar experiences. The American novelist John Dos
Passos, whose Spanish translator Jose Robles had been murdered
by the Communist secret police, wrote that he had

> come to believe that the Communist Party is funda-
> mentally opposed to our democracy as I see it and that
> Marxism, though an important basis for the unborn
> sociological sciences, if held as a dogma, is a reac-
> tionary force and an impediment to progress. Fascism
> is nothing but Marxism inside out and is of course
> a worse impediment—but the old argument about
> giving aid and comfort to the enemy is rubbish: free
> thought can't possibly give aid and comfort to fas-
> cism . . . I now think that foreign liberals and radicals
> were very wrong not to protest against the Russian ter-
> ror all down the line.

It takes only a glance at 'Looking Back on the Spanish War', a long,
reminiscing essay written in 1942, to establish the extraordinary
impact that Spain had on Orwell. It was here, for the first time
in his life, that he had seen a totalitarian regime in action, not
only bent on liquidating its enemies—there was even a Spanish
Communist Party poster emblazoned with the image of a boot
stamping 'on all who resist forever'—but manipulating the past

to ensure that its own version of history would be the one that survived. It was in Spain, as he later acknowledged, that he read newspaper articles that bore no relation to the known facts and saw troops whom he knew to have fought valiantly denounced as cowards and traitors. It was in Spain, too, that he caught the first warning signs of a phenomenon that would oppress him until the end of his life, a suspicion that the idea of objective truth was 'falling out of the world'. In the future, he believed, history books would simply reflect the prejudices of whomever happened to be in power. Despite a residual attachment to the rituals of the Anglican church, Orwell was not a religious man. On the other hand, he was keen to suggest that the rise of totalitarianism was directly linked to the fact that an increasing number of people no longer believed in an afterlife. 'The major problem of our time is the decay of belief in personal immortality', he wrote. The autocrat who no longer feared divine judgement or assumed that whatever happened to the world after he died no longer matters could do what he liked.

Spain, it is safe to say, politicised Orwell. Like Dos Passos, he remained on the Left while sharply critical of the Left's intolerance of dissent and its frequent insistence that the end justified the means. Here in the build-up to the Second World War, he saw the consequences of the moral duplicity that lay at its core everywhere he looked: in the editors and publishers who, he believed, rejected books and articles that peddled inconvenient truths about the way the conflict had been fought and the personal enmities brought back by veterans with bitter personal experience of faction fighting. There was a spectacular falling out with his own publisher, Victor Gollancz, who had insisted in 1937 that 'support of the Soviet Union at the present juncture is . . . of such overwhelming importance that anything that can be quoted by the other side should not be said': *Homage to Catalonia* was eventually published by the rival firm of Secker & Warburg. During the period 1937–9 the memory of Spain was everywhere in Orwell's life: in the books he reviewed, in the friendships he kept up, in the journalism he wrote attempting to correct misrepresentations of the war in the English press, and, unhappily, in his shattered health. The succession of freezing nights spent on guard duty on the Aragon Front had further undermined an already frail constitution: he was seriously ill in the spring of 1938, and spent nearly six months in a sanatorium and a further seven convalescing in Morocco. 'Looking Back on the Spanish War', written four years after the conflict came to an end, is a kind of creative bridging point, simultaneously returning to an episode of enormous emotional and political significance and looking forward to the horrors of *Nineteen Eighty-Four*.

THE ROOTS of Orwell's obsession with the totalitarian mind are strewn all over his life in the late 1930s and the early 1940s. Naturally, they can be found in the books he read and in the books he wrote himself, but they would also have been sharply apparent in some of the international news that sprang each morning from the pages of his daily newspaper. In the third category, he would certainly have taken an interest in the widely reported Soviet show trials of 1938, which led to the deaths of erstwhile pillars of the regime such as Genrikh Yagoda, Alexei Rykoff, and Nikolai Bukharin, and of which *The Times*'s special correspondent in Moscow remarked: 'According to Soviet law, crime and the intent to commit crime are virtually the same thing . . . In the coming trial the prosecution expects to show that the accused premeditated certain crimes though they never committed them—and therefore are little less guilty than if the crimes had actually been committed'. It was in 1938, too, that he read Eugene Lyons's *Assignment in Utopia*, a memoir by the United Press Agency's Moscow correspondent from 1928 to 1934, with its incriminating reportage from a world in which the leader's portrait hung in every apartment, children denounced their parents as traitors, and even making an inappropriate gesture could lead to arrest and imprisonment.

But all this is to ignore Orwell's growing interest in the burgeoning genre of dystopian literature—novels set in imaginary never-never lands where something has gone badly wrong, usually in a way that amplifies some of the political tendencies of the world in which it was written. It is more than likely, for example, that Orwell read Murray Constantine's *Swastika Night* (1937)—it was published by Gollancz and, like *The Road to Wigan Pier*, was chosen for the Left Book Club—which envisages a world tyrannised over by the Nazis for the past 700 years, where German and Japanese empires squabble incessantly over their colonial possessions. There are several eerie little prefigurations of *Nineteen Eighty-Four*, from the dissident hero's discovery that there had in the past existed such things as 'memory' and 'socialism', to the demonization of the four 'archfiends' (these include Lenin and Stalin), which might be thought to predate the Inner Party's treatment of Emmanuel Goldstein. None of which proves that Orwell read it, but the eagerness with which he sought out and drew attention to dystopian fiction that he thought relevant to contemporary political systems is a point in its favour.

Pride of place in this catalogue of formative influences is occupied by a round-up review that Orwell contributed to the weekly magazine *Time and Tide* in July 1940, shortly after the fall of France, which he would have sat down to write in the realisation that Britain might very shortly be invaded. The four books chosen to illustrate his thesis are Jack London's *The Iron Heel* (1908), H.G. Wells's *When the Sleeper Wakes* (1907), Aldous Huxley's *Brave New World* (1932), and Ernest Bramah's *The Secret of the League* (1907)—each set in a dystopia and each indirectly connected to the way in which *Nineteen Eighty-Four* would come to be conceived. The significance of the piece lies in Orwell's analysis of the four alternate worlds on display and his attempt to establish their plausibility. According to this estimate, *The Iron Heel*, in which a band of robber barons supported by a private army known as 'the mercenaries' wrests control of America, is not a forecast of Fascism but 'merely a tale of capitalist oppression'. At the same time, he makes a distinction between London and Wells: 'because of his own streak of savagery London could grasp something that Wells apparently could not, and that is that hedonistic societies do not endure'.

When the Sleeper Wakes, he maintains, offers a vision of a glittering, sinister world, with a permanently enslaved workforce, expressly designed to allow a soft, amoral upper class to amuse itself. *Brave New World*, written a quarter of a century later, with its pleasure domes and constant pursuit of sensual gratification, is a kind of parody of these political arrangements, in which 'the whole world has turned into a Riviera hotel'. This may be a wonderful caricature of the upper-bourgeois world of 1930, Orwell hastens to explain, but it is not prophetic.

No society of that kind would last more than a couple of generations, because a ruling class which thought principally in terms of a 'good time' would soon lose its vitality. A ruling class has got to have a strict morality, a quasi-religious belief in itself, a mystique.

Jack London's land-grabbing plutocrats might be tyrants and swindlers, but they are not sensualists or idlers. They maintain their position because they honestly believe that civilisation depends on them. The same, nine years later, is true of the appa-ratchiks of *Nineteen Eighty-Four*. Every crime the members of the Inner Party commit is necessary—not that they would regard their activities as criminal—for in their absence, and without their decisive intervention, the world would instantly be reduced to chaos.

All this represents an important step in Orwell's under-standing of the totalitarian mindset and, in particular, its mys-tical and well-nigh religious underpinning. It was not only that the mid-twentieth century's flight from God had created a vast reservoir of displaced religious sensibility; it had also provided a key ingredient of the atmosphere in which totalitarian soci-eties took root and flourished. 'Inside the Whale', a long essay from 1940, subtitled 'Writers and Leviathan', picks up this theme: the Western world is moving into a time of 'totalitarian dicta-torships', Orwell argues, when freedom of thought will become first a 'deadly sin' and in the end little more than a 'meaningless abstraction'. A later review of Malcolm Muggeridge's *The Thir-ties* contrasts the processes of thought control exercised by the Catholic Church with the depredations of the totalitarian state.

If supernatural sanctions no longer apply, then people have a licence to do as they believe without fear of punishment. In all likelihood, the future will consist of a secular version of the Spanish Inquisition, made yet more powerful by radio transmissions and secret police surveillance.

As to where all this left England, here in the first year of war, *The Lion and the Unicorn: Socialism and the English Genius*, a long essay published in pamphlet form in 1941, is relatively optimistic. Only a socialist nation could fight effectively, Orwell proposed. By turning itself into one, by democratising its institutions, tearing down the bastions of privilege, and fostering greater equality—by saying goodbye to the old lady in the Rolls Royce car, as he figuratively put it—England might be able to bring off a trick that no European nation had yet managed to achieve: centralising its economy while preserving the freedom of its citizens. Meanwhile, wherever one looks in Orwell's life, the situational details on which *Nineteen Eighty-Four* would rely are beginning to stack up. Eileen's first wartime job took her to the Censorship Department in Whitehall, where she and her colleagues decided which homegrown newspapers and magazines were suitable for export and issued 'stop' notices prohibiting correspondents from neutral countries filing stories which contained sensitive material. Naturally, the news coming in from Nazi-occupied Europe brought constant reminders of the way in which objective truth seemed to be falling out of the world. A diary entry from June 1942, for example, notes that

> the Germans announce over the wireless that as the inhabitants of a Czech village called Ladice [Lidice] (about 1200 inhabitants) were guilty of harbouring the

assassins of Heydrich they have shot all the males in
the village, sent all the women to concentration camps,
sent all the children to be 're-educated', razed the whole
village to the ground and changed its name.

Wartime atrocities, Orwell concluded, were to be 'believed in or
disbelieved in according to political predilection, with utter non-
interest in the facts and with complete willingness to alter one's
beliefs as soon as the political scene alters'. Other twitches on the
prefigurative thread were from closer to home. By this stage, the
Orwells had come to rest at Langford Court, an apartment block
on Abbey Road in St John's Wood, London NW8. Here, like Winston Smith, they occupied a single-bedroom flat on the seventh
floor, with a view looking out over central London in sight of
the Ministry of Information's headquarters at the University of
London's Senate House—a vast, sinister skyscraper whose upper
stories looked out over the war-torn city and whose countless
windows dazzled in the morning sun. The building's telegraphic
address was *miniform* (compare the Newspeak word for the Ministry of Truth, *Minitrue*) while its director, Churchill's protégé
Brendan Bracken, was known to his subordinates as 'BB'.

And then there was the job Orwell held down as a producer
for the Indian Section of the BBC's Eastern Service between mid-
1941 and the latter part of 1943, scripting and recording broadcasts for Anglophone audiences in South East Asia. Almost from
the outset, Orwell discounted the value of his work for the BBC.
Six months into his time there he suggested that the atmosphere
was 'something halfway between a girls' school and a lunatic
asylum' and that 'all we are doing at present is useless or slightly
worse than useless'. Later he would mark the experience down as

'two wasted years'. But however great his sense of frustration and dislike of BBC protocols, there was a way in which the cramped interiors and punctiliously observed daily routines worked on his mind. One of his tasks was to script the Section's weekly news broadcasts with their updates on the progress of the war. Six years later, Winston will see in his mind a map of the fighting with arrows sweeping across India showing the defeat of the Eurasian forces. Moreover, Orwell was essentially being employed as a propagandist, even if, as he once put it, 'while here I consider that I have kept our propaganda slightly less disgusting than it might otherwise have been . . . To appreciate this you have to be as I am in constant touch with propaganda Axis and Allied. Till then you don't realise what muck and filth is flowing through the air'.

His duties took place in the Corporation's premises at 200 Oxford Street, whose rows of hutch-like offices and dismal canteen look as if they contributed something to Winston's daily routines at the Ministry of Truth, while the room at the BBC headquarters in Portland Place where Eastern Service editorial meetings took place was numbered 101. One of Orwell's closest colleagues was the literary critic William Empson, an enthusiast for the 'Basic English' techniques pioneered by Professor C.K. Ogden and, as such, a more than plausible candidate for the original of *Nineteen Eighty-Four*'s Newspeak-obsessed Syme. And there is a revealing diary entry from the early days of his employment:

The only time when one hears people singing in the B.B.C. is in the early morning between 6 and 8. That is the time when the charwomen are at work. A huge army of them arrives all at the same time. They sit in the reception hall waiting for their brooms to be issued to them and making as much noise as a parrot house, and then they have wonderful choruses, all singing together as they sweep the passages. The place has a quite different atmosphere at this time from what it has later in the day.

Several critics have taken this to be the origin of the prole woman on whom Winston and Julia eavesdrop from the window of their room above Mr Charrington's shop, singing a popular song of the day as she pegs out laundry on a line. The woman, who marches 'to and fro, corking and uncorking herself, singing and falling silent, and pegging out more diapers, and more and yet more', is never named, but the role she plays in *Nineteen Eighteen-Four* is highly symbolic. Watching her going uncomplainingly about her work, Winston feels a 'mystical reverence', which is somehow mixed up with the pale, cloudless sky that stretches away over her head.

It was curious to think that the sky was the same for everybody, in Eurasia or Eastasia as well as here. And the people under the sky were also very much the same—everywhere, all over the world, hundreds and thousands and millions of people just like this, people ignorant of one another's existence, held apart by walls of hatred and lies, and yet almost exactly the same—people who had never learned to think but were storing up in their hearts and bellies and muscles the power that would one day overturn the world.

If there was hope, Winston decides, it lay in the proles. Without yet having reached the end of *The Theory and Practice of Oligarchical Collectivism*, he knows instinctively that this must be Goldstein's final message.

All these influences add up. By the autumn of 1943, as the war entered its fifth year and the Anglo-American forces assembling in the Home Counties geared up for the launch of a Second Front in Nazi-occupied France, most of the materials on which *Nineteen Eighty-Four* would come to depend had taken up residence in Orwell's imagination. All that was needed now was a spark to set them aflame.

PART II

During (1943–1949)

4. FITS AND STARTS

AT LEAST THREE of Orwell's novels can be tracked back to the particular image or thought process that inspired their conception. With *Animal Farm*, it was the sight of a small boy escorting a giant cart horse down a country lane and the thought of what might happen if the animal world rose up against its human oppressors. *Keep the Aspidistra Flying* looks as if it began life at the moment on St Andrew's Day 1934 when Orwell stared out of the window of the Hampstead bookshop in which he worked and found the first fragments of the poem whose composition occupies its opening chapter ('Sharply the menacing wind sweeps o'er / The bending poplars, newly bare') taking shape in his head. *Nineteen Eighty-Four*, on the other hand, took its impetus from a hugely significant political event—the Tehran Conference of 28 November to 1 December 1943, in which, with the end of the Second World War in sight, the Allied leaders Roosevelt, Stalin, and Churchill sat down with the aim of carving up the post-war world. 'I first thought of it in 1943', Orwell told his publisher, Fred Warburg, nearly five years later, although a later note to Warburg's associate, Roger Senhouse, suggests that there was a slight delay between the event itself and the seed of a novel taking root in Orwell's mind. Here, after complaining that the jacket copy blurb Senhouse has devised makes the novel sound like a thriller mixed up with a love story, Orwell insists that 'What it is really meant to do is to discuss the implications of dividing the world up into "Zones of Influence" (I thought of it in 1944 as a result of the Tehran Conference), & in addition to indicate by parodying them the intellectual implications of totalitarianism'.

But if the pictures of 'the big three', as the Allied leaders were known, battling for territorial precedence gave Orwell the creative nudge he needed, then there is a suspicion that much of the background to *Nineteen Eighty-Four* had been taking shape in his mind for several years. One of the most intriguing items in the Orwell Archive at University College London is an exercise book containing notes for two projected novels entitled 'The Quick and the Dead' and 'The Last Man in Europe'. The first set of jottings looks back to the world of Orwell's childhood—there are references to Charing Cross Station in the last year of the Great War and a dying horse in 'the retreat in 1918' and lists of old rhymes, 'childhood fallacies', and folk-sayings—but 'The Last Man in Europe' (*Nineteen Eighty-Four*'s working title until at least the end of 1948) is instantly recognisable. Under the heading *To be brought in*, for example, Orwell has reminded himself about 'Newspeak', 'position of the proles', 'comparison of weights, measures etc', 'Bakerism & ingsoc', 'the party slogans (War is Peace, Ignorance is Strength, Freedom is Slavery)', and 'The Two Minutes Hate'.

Beneath this runs a long section of notes headed *The general lay-out as follows*. This includes 'The system of organised lying on which society is founded', 'The way in which this is done (falsification of records etc)', 'The nightmare feeling caused by the disappearance of objective truth', 'Leader-worship etc', and 'Loneliness of the writer. His feeling of being *the last man*', 'The brief interlude of the love affair with Y', and 'The arrest & torture'. There is also mention of 'the phantasmagorical effect' produced by such questions as 'Were we at war with Eastasia in 1974? Were we at war with Eastasia in 1978? Were A, B & C present at the secret conference in 1976?' and 'the effect of lies & hatred' produced by such phenomena as 'Films. Extract of anti-Jew propaganda. B'casts' and 'The Two Minutes Hate. Enemy propaganda & writer's response to it'. A final section, which lists words under the headings 'Adjectives', 'Adjectives & nouns', 'Metaphors', 'Metaphorical words & phrases', 'Redundancies', and 'Stale slang & jargon phrases', looks as if it is a dry run for some of the obfuscations of Newspeak and ends with a file of phrases whose real definition represents a 180-degree turn from the original ('People's democracy . . . One party dictatorship. Acceptance in principle . . . refusal', etc.).

When were the notebooks compiled? There is a strong suspicion that some of the material in them dates back to the early part of the war, as an autobiographical note from April 1940 states that Orwell is 'projecting a long novel in three parts to be called either "The Lion & the Unicorn" or "The Quick and the Dead"'. They are unlikely to have been completed later than January 1944, as Orwell refers to the list of 'childhood fallacies' ('That dogs are good judges of character/That snakes sting', etc.) which he claims in one of his *Tribune* essays to have 'in a notebook'. The final 'Newspeak' section is written using a blue-black Biro, a writing implement not available in the UK until after the war: Orwell first ordered one in February 1946. Clearly the first two sections predate this, but by how long? Were they set down as an outline of future schemes as he prepared to leave the BBC in the autumn of 1943? Or during the fortnight's holiday that we know him to have taken in September? Alternatively, are they simply a fair copy of existing material which Orwell has now decided to get into some kind of coherent order? Certainly, the notes are neatly written, devoid of crossings out or repetitions. As literary preliminaries go, they look more like parts of an outline than a series of random jottings. None of this is conclusive, but it would seem that by the autumn of 1943, having brooded on the material for some time—perhaps as long as three or four years—Orwell had produced a ground plan of what became *Nineteen Eighty-Four* and that the Tehran Conference gave his consciousness a decisive kick.

Whatever the dating of Orwell's notes for 'The Last Man in Europe', and for however long its central themes had been crowding out his imagination, by the spring of 1944, we can see his mind beginning to focus on what he believed to be the defining characteristics of the totalitarian state. In early February, for example, the 'As I Please' column that he had begun to contribute to the left-wing weekly magazine *Tribune* suggests that totalitarianism's most terrifying quality is not only that it instigates atrocities, but that it seeks to control 'the concept of objective truth' and thereby manipulates both past and future. A few weeks later, he produced an *Observer* review of F.A. Hayek's *The Road to Serfdom*, shortly to become a key text in the canon of the post-war Right. While Orwell profoundly disagreed with Hayek's defence of the free market ('he does not see, or will not admit, that a return to "free" competition means for the great mass of people a tyranny probably worse . . . than that of the State'), he feared that its central thesis—that collectivism is inherently undemocratic—had a great deal of truth: 'By bringing the whole of life under the control of the State, Socialism necessarily gives power to an inner ring of bureaucrats, who in almost every case will be men who want power for its own sake and will stick at nothing in order to retain it'.

Significantly, these concerns soon began to leach into his private correspondence with readers who had responded to his newspaper columns or wanted his views on the probable shape of the post-war world. In May 1944, three weeks before the British and American armies landed on the Normandy coast, he wrote a long letter to an otherwise unidentified man named Noel Willmett predicting that while 'Hitler, no doubt, will soon disappear', his overthrow will come at the expense of strengthening '(a) Stalin, (b) the Anglo-American millionaires and (c) all sorts of petty fuhrers'. Everywhere in the world, 'movement' seems to be in the direction of centralised economies, which may deliver the goods in an economic sense but do so without regard to democratic accountability.

> With this go the horrors of emotional nationalism and a tendency to disbelieve in the existence of objective truth because all the facts have to fit in with the words and prophecies of some infallible fuhrer. Already history has in a sense ceased to exist, ie, there is no such thing as a history of our own times which could be universally accepted, and the exact sciences are endangered as soon as military necessity ceases to keep people up to the mark.

This is a private letter, written in the month before D-Day, nearly a year before the Second World War had come to an end, but already the shadows of Big Brother, the Two Minutes Hate, and the Ministry of Truth are crowding in from all sides.

Then, in the summer of 1944, came another twitch on the conceptual thread. Late in August, Orwell attended a conference organised by the international writers' association PEN. Here he listened to, and was impressed by, a lecture by the Oxford biologist John R. Baker. At first glance, Baker looks an unlikely focus for Orwell's admiration. He was a conservatively minded social scientist, active in the Society for Freedom in Science, and later the author of a highly reactionary book on race, who believed that his discipline was a useful weapon in the fight against protest movements of the egalitarian left. Nevertheless, Orwell mentions him favourably in a review of a symposium to which Baker had contributed in October 1945, read his book *Science and the Planned State* sometime in the following spring, and seems to have wanted to involve him in a scheme to establish a pressure group bent on defending individual freedom. A letter to Arthur Koestler survives from April 1946 in which Orwell suggests that Baker might be 'useful' in coming up with information about scientists who are 'not totalitarian minded'.

It is not known whether Orwell made contact with Baker at the PEN conference, but he certainly attended his lecture. This developed one of *Science and the Planned State*'s key arguments, which is that scientific research cannot flourish under the rule of a bureaucracy, if only because the fruits of that research may undermine the bureaucracy's ideological position. State interference, Baker insisted, was a challenge to scientific freedom ('The scientist's most fundamental liberty is threatened to-day by the would-be central planners of the subject'). His particular bugbear was the Soviet scientist Trofim Denisovich Lysenko, who in his capacity as director of the Soviet Academy of Agricultural Science, rejected the findings of Western genetics and demanded that Soviet researchers adopt his beliefs. Anti-Mendel—there was no such thing as a 'gene', Lysenko maintained—and rejecting

Darwin's theories of natural selection, Lysenko's paralysing influence on Russian science lasted for something over twenty years. Warmly approved of by Stalin and the Soviet hierarchy, which in 1948 declared his views 'the only correct theory', his opponents denounced in the press as 'bourgeois' and 'fascists', he was indirectly responsible for the execution of dozens of Soviet scientists and imprisonment of several thousand more. 'Lysenkoism' remained a force in Eastern European scientific circles until at least the end of the 1950s. Lysenko's rise to power offered 'a vivid illustration of the degradation of science under a totalitarian regime', Baker concluded.

Orwell continued to be fascinated by the Lysenko case and its implications for academic study. A letter from March 1947 to the botanist Cyril Darlington, known since his days as a BBC talks producer, notes that 'I first heard about it in the speech given by John Baker at the PEN Conference in 1944 . . . I formed the opinion then that the story as told by Baker was true and am very glad to get this confirmation'. He was no scientist, Orwell admitted, but the Soviet Union's persecution of scientists and its falsification of results seemed to follow naturally from its attacks on writers and historians. His interest in the duplicities of Soviet science kept up almost until the month of his death, and his last literary notebook contains a press cutting from December 1949 which quoted Lysenko as maintaining that 'Wheat can become Rye'. That Orwell found himself sitting in Baker's audience in August 1944 was clearly a pivotal moment to him. Among other things, it may explain a hitherto mysterious reference in the outline of the 'The Last Man in Europe' to 'the swindle of Bakerism and Ingsoc'. 'Ingsoc' is a truncation of 'English Socialism', Oceania's ideological creed, but 'Bakerism' looks as if it tracks back to

John Baker. Here, in the reality-denying of the Soviet Academy of Agricultural Science, another fragment of *Nineteen Eighty-Four*'s mosaic fits neatly into place.

It was now the early autumn of 1944. Orwell had a conceptual spark, a theme, and a mounting pile of evidence that could be used to illustrate it. What stayed his hand? One of the most obvious questions to ask about *Nineteen Eighty-Four*'s gestation is: what took him so long? The pre-war Orwell had been known for his fluency: most of the books he wrote in the period 1932–9 had occupied him for less than a year. *A Clergyman's Daughter*, written at his parents' house in Southwold while he was convalescing from a bout of pneumonia, had taken a little over six months. *Animal Farm*—only 120 pages in length, admittedly, but tricky from the point of view of plot and alignment with the historical events it pastiched—was finished in half that time. Compared to these high-speed dashes to the finishing tape, *Nineteen Eighty-Four* was a marathon: a few pages written by the end of 1945; a first draft not completed until November 1947; a second draft not wrapped up until December 1948; publication not secured until June 1949; a whole five-and-a-half years gone by since the moment Orwell had read the press reports of Roosevelt, Churchill, and Stalin caballing at Tehran. What went wrong?

The answer lies in a combination of personal and professional factors, a series of obstacles strewn across Orwell's life in the mid-1940s that stopped a once-prolific author from working on the book he burned to write. The most immediate problem was the future of *Animal Farm*, finished by the early spring of 1944 but, such was its highly contentious subject matter, very nearly not published at all. Even Orwell might have conceded that its timing was, to say the least, unfortunate. Here, after all, was a satirical fantasy whose subject was the betrayal of the Russian Revolution of 1917 by a gang of corrupt and authoritarian leaders, completed at exactly the moment when Britain and America's gallant Soviet allies were preparing for an assault on Berlin. Orwell's fiction was still under contract to Victor Gollancz, but Gollancz, having inspected the manuscript, could not bring himself to publish it. The firm of Nicholson & Watson said the same. A third publishing house, Jonathan Cape, was persuaded to reject it on the advice of an official from the Ministry of Information (later unmasked as a Communist spy), on the grounds that the flagrant anti-Soviet basis was unacceptable. All through the summer of 1944, the novel's fate hung in the balance—at one point, Orwell grew so desperate that he was prepared to publish it himself in pamphlet form—and it was not until the early autumn that Secker & Warburg agreed to publish it. Even then, paper shortages delayed its appearance until the summer of 1945.

Secker's decision to acquire the novel re-united Orwell with Fred Warburg, who had published *Homage to Catalonia* back in 1938 and sponsored the pamphlet-sized *The Lion and the Unicorn* three years later. A distant cousin of the great American tycoons Felix and Paul, Warburg had bought up the moribund firm of Martin Secker in 1936 for a few thousand pounds, added his own name to it, and secured his first big success with an English translation of Gabriel Chevallier's novel *Clochemerle* (1937). But however stylish and newsworthy Warburg's list, Secker was still a small and precariously financed concern: in allowing his books to be published by them, Orwell was taking a risk. Happily, his— and Warburg's—gamble paid off. *Animal Farm* was a considerable success. Four and a half thousand copies were sold in the six weeks following publication, and a reprint of 10,000 ordered for October. The Queen herself demanded a copy, and a royal messenger, finding all the major London outlets sold out, was forced to call at the anarchist bookshop run by Orwell's friend George Woodcock.

But this professional success was accompanied, and to a large extent undermined, by a private life lived out amid the chaos of wartime London. Come mid-1944, the Orwells were living in Islington, after a flying bomb had fallen on their previous address in Kilburn. By this time, Orwell and his wife Eileen had been married for eight years. Orwell always blamed their childlessness on what he believed was his own 'sterility', but a likelier explanation can be found in Eileen's growing ill health. She had been unwell, on and off, for most of the war: friends noted her tiredness and general air of exhaustion. In the summer of 1944, with the help of her sister-in-law, who worked as a doctor in the Newcastle area, they decided to adopt a child. Richard Horatio Blair, as the baby was subsequently christened, born on 14 May 1944, arrived at the Islington flat. 'Life is pretty full up now', Orwell told his friend Rayner Heppenstall. But Eileen, though enraptured by the baby, pleased to have given up her wartime job, and full of enthusiasm for her new role (she 'wanted to live' again, her husband explained), was still unwell with what a medical examination revealed to be tumours on the uterus. Taken into hospital in March 1945 for what was alleged to be a 'routine' operation to remove them, Eileen suffered heart failure and died on the operating table.

The effect on Orwell, then temporarily employed as a foreign correspondent for the *Observer* in Occupied Europe, was devastating. Many a writer in his position—in poor health and with a bulging work book—would have given up on his dreams of parenthood, but he was determined to carry his plan of raising a child through to fulfilment by hiring a nanny and actively involving himself in the routines of Richard's daily life. Still, though, the trauma of Eileen's death lingered. One of its consequences, in the winter of 1945–6, was Orwell's habit of proposing marriage, more or less on the spot and without encouragement, to any remotely eligible woman who came his way: a girl who lived in the same apartment block and barely knew him was startled to receive an invitation to tea and then be cornered on the sofa with the words 'Do you think you could take care of me?' None of these proposals came to anything—however sympathetic, the girls were usually unwilling to become romantically involved—but they reinforce the impression, common to Orwell's friends in the post-Eileen period, of an unhappy man whose life had run irretrievably out of kilter.

Widowed, exhausted, and emotionally distraught, Orwell was in no condition to begin work on a new book. On the other hand, without openly acknowledging the fact, he was keen to discuss its themes with friends. Many of the visitors to Canonbury Square who had listened to him dilating on the state of the post-war world were subsequently able to recognise that they had been attending to embryonic versions of *Nineteen Eighty-Four*: George Woodcock reckoned that these long tea-table conversations had introduced to him all the basic ideas years before he saw the book in print. A brief flurry of work in the summer of 1945 was quickly abandoned (a Secker & Warburg internal memorandum dated 25 June 1945 states that 'George Orwell has written the first twelve pages of his novel, but of course disclaims knowledge of when it will be finished'.) The opening passages of *Nineteen Eighty-Four*'s first draft, probably sketched out at this time, depict

Winston Smith trying to make his way into Victory Mansions. Here he is confronted by an aged porter with 'a grey, seamed face' who announces that 'Lift ain't working'. They have little of the final version's attack.

Meanwhile, there was another factor liable to get in the way of any literary schemes. This was the serious illness Orwell suffered in early 1946, revealed at the moment when Richard's nanny, Susan Watson, hard at work in the kitchen but disturbed by noises elsewhere in the Islington flat, found her employer staggering down the passage with blood pouring from his mouth. What happened next was an eerily symbolic demonstration of Orwell's commitment to his work. To Susan—instantly commanded to fetch a jug of iced water and a block of ice from the Frigidaire—it was obvious that he had suffered a tubercular haemorrhage. But to have admitted to TB would have meant immediate hospitalisation. Consequently, by the time the doctor arrived, Orwell had staunched the flow of blood, concealed himself beneath the bed covers and, by lying through his teeth, was able to pass the illness off as a bad attack of gastritis. He spent the next fortnight in bed, pretending to friends that he was suffering from a severe stomach complaint—'quite an unpleasant thing to have, but I am somewhat better and got up for the first time today', he told one of the girls he had asked to marry him a month or so before.

All this gives the initial stages of Nineteen Eighty-Four's composition an unignorable context. It is fair to say that the man who wrote the novel was physically undermined by years of overwork and illness and gravely traumatised by his wife's death. At the same time, Orwell had also taken the first steps to dislodge himself from the environment in which he had spent most of the war years. As early as September 1944 he had paid his first visit to

Jura, the Inner Hebridean island that was to become his base for much of the rest of his life. There was a second trip in the autumn of 1945, and by the end of the year, helped by his friend David Astor, who knew the landlord, he had arranged to rent a remote farmhouse named Barnhill on the island's northernmost tip. Opinions differ over the impulse that sent Orwell several hundred miles north of London to a corner of Scotland so detached from the amenities of civilised life that the road ran out eight miles before visitors came in sight of the property. To Anthony Powell it was a reaction to the success of *Animal Farm* and the fear of becoming conspicuous. Other friends remembered Orwell talking of the threat of nuclear holocaust and his conviction that Richard would be safer in the far north. To set against these recollections is a diary entry from as far back as June 1940, which finds Orwell 'thinking always of my island in the Hebrides, which I suppose I shall never possess nor even see'. Whatever the explanation, Jura soon become another factor in *Nineteen Eighty-Four*'s development. The next three years of Orwell's life follow an ever-narrower pattern: journeys back and forth from the Inner Hebrides; brooding over *Nineteen Eighty-Four*; prodigious amounts of newspaper and magazine commissions (the autumn of 1946 was taken up by a torrent of journalistic work); and growing debility.

But there was one more book he needed to read before the novel's scheme would become clear in his head. In a *Tribune* column from early January 1946 entitled 'Freedom and Happiness', he announces that he has 'at last got my hands' on a copy of Yevgeny Zamyatin's *We*, a legendary dystopian fantasy of the twenty-sixth century written in the early 1920s by a Russian citizen but suppressed in the USSR and available only in English, French, and Czech translations. Part of the interest in Orwell's essay rests on the fact that he doubts whether the Soviet regime is the main target: 'What Zamyatin seems to be aiming at is not any particular country but the implied aim of industrial society'. On the other hand, 'Utopia', whose cowed inhabitants are so de-individualised that they are known only by numbers, bears several resemblances to Oceania. Controlled by a potentate known as the 'Benefactor', tyrannised over by a politicised police force known as the 'Guardians', and compelling its citizens to march in fours while the anthem of the Single State is played through a loudspeaker, Zamyatin's alternate world is based on the idea that happiness and freedom are incompatible. Inner serenity is achievable only by doing what you are told.

This template is shattered by *We*'s anonymous hero, D-503, who falls in love with I-330. In the rebellion that follows, the authorities announce that its cause is the fact that certain human beings suffer from a disease called imagination. Later, D-503 watches without emotion as I-330 is tortured. The rebels are publicly executed.

Zamyatin continued to interest Orwell. Nearly three years later, only a week or so before *Nineteen Eighty-Four* was complete, he wrote to Fred Warburg with the news that a British publishing firm booked to bring out a translation had gone bankrupt and wondering if Secker & Warburg would like to take it over ('It is quite a remarkable book. It was no doubt suppressed by the Russian authorities because they thought it was a satire on themselves, but I should say it was more a satire on Utopianism generally, and incidentally I think Aldous Huxley's "Brave New World" was partly plagiarised from it'). And while there are several dystopian fictions with some kind of recognisable influence on *Nineteen Eighty-Four*, it is significant that his first real assault on the novel came three or four months after he had first been introduced to Zamyatin.

Significantly, the *Tribune* essay appeared only a day after the first stirrings of a tendency that would characterise the next three years' work on *Nineteen Eighty-Four*: Orwell's habit of seizing on tiny pieces of detail from his everyday life and incorporating them into the text. In 'Just Junk—But Who Could Resist It?', a short piece written for the *London Evening Standard*, Orwell reminisces about the pleasure to be found from visiting central London's second-hand shops. Some of the things to look out for, he instructs his readers, are 'Victorian brooches and lockets of agate or other semi-precious stones'. A paragraph or two later he mentions 'glass paperweights with pictures at the bottom', going on to warn, 'There are others that have a piece of coral enclosed in the glass, but these are always fantastically expensive'. From here it is only a short, imaginative step to Mr Charrington's antique shop with its 'lacquered snuff-boxes, agate brooches and the like' and the scene in which Winston, puzzled by a 'strange, pink, convoluted object that recalled a rose or a sea anemone', is told that this is a piece of coral, and pays the shop owner four dollars for the joy of sliding 'the coveted thing into his pocket'. If much of *Nineteen Eighty-Four* is conjured out of nowhere, then many of its incidental fragments turn out to have been robbed wholesale from the life that ran along beside it.

5. JURA DAYS

ORWELL SET OFF FOR SCOTLAND at the end of May 1946 to take possession of his new domain. By early July, Barnhill's population had expanded to include his sister Avril, the young Richard—by now a week or so past his second birthday—and Susan Watson, Richard's nanny. His original plan had been to start work on the novel as soon as the house had been put in some kind of order, but the domestic arrangements took time and the summer weather was a distraction. Friends came to stay; Richard had to be fetched from London; there was a trip to Glasgow to collect Susan's small daughter. At the same time, always keen on 'nature' and the advantages of the outdoor world, Orwell was deeply absorbed in the life of Jura: the domestic notebooks that he began to keep at this time are full of enraptured accounts of the local bird population, or the difficulties involved in hauling a stranded cow out of a bog. Progress was slow—in late September, on the point of returning to London, he confessed to his friend Hugh Slater that 'I haven't really done any work this summer—actually I have at last started a novel about the future, but I've only done about 50 pages and God knows when it will be finished'—and incremental. Even now, the pile of manuscript sheets slowly accumulating in the study bedroom lacked a definite title—although he continued to favour 'The Last Man in Europe'—and there were attempts to establish it in 1980 and 1982 before he finally settled on 1984.

Unbeknown to its author, the first draft of what became *Nineteen Eighty-Four* had two early readers. These were Susan Watson and her visiting boyfriend, a 23-year-old Cambridge graduate named David Holbrook, who amused themselves by sneaking upstairs while Orwell was out of the house and taking surreptitious glances at the work-in-progress. Holbrook, although a fan of Orwell's early books , was unimpressed. 'Pretty depressing stuff', he later recalled. 'There was this man Winston . . . and these dismal sexual episodes. It just seemed depressingly lacking in hope'. For his own part, Orwell was deeply suspicious of Holbrook, a self-declared Communist who, he suspected, had been sent north by the party commissars to spy on him. Holbrook's involvement with Susan was a further bone of contention. Later the younger man would write a merciless, though unpublished, autobiographical novel in which Orwell features as a writer named 'Gregory Burwell'—tall, mournful, and chronically self-absorbed, and pictured by Holbrook's alter ego enjoying long, miserable conversations with his sister 'Olwyn' ('The couple's gloomiest pleasure was in undermining all possibilities: they liked everything to be inaccessible, broken beyond repair, unattainable. There was no help to be had, no support, no community, no human succour'.).

It was not only the diversions of a Hebridean summer that hindered Orwell's work on the book. To the temptation to put down his pen and take Richard for a walk around the Barnhill estate or shoot one of the establishment's geese for the communal supper could be added the fact that much of *Nineteen Eighty-Four*'s structure was still taking shape in his mind. Much of the journalism he wrote in 1945–6 shows him exploring themes that would later resurface in the novel slowly gestating on the study desk. Several essays from this time, for example, find him brooding about the likely geographical dimensions of the post-war world. In 'You and the Atom Bomb', written for *Tribune* in October 1945, only a couple of months after the nuclear strikes on Hiroshima and Nagasaki, he suggests that 'More and more obviously the surface of the earth is being parcelled off into three great empires, each self-contained and cut off from contact with the outer world, and each ruled, under one disguise or other, by a self-elected oligarchy'. The haggling is still going on and the third of the three land blocs—East Asia dominated by China—is potential rather than actual, but the tendency is unmistakable. The atomic bomb may complete this process by robbing the exploited classes of their power to revolt and putting the people who own the bomb on a basis of military equality.

A second essay, about the American management guru James Burnham, published in the month Orwell arrived on Jura, expands some of these ideas. In particular, its opening summary of Burnham's book, *The Managerial Revolution*, seems directly related to the minutely regulated, highly centralised, and above all oligarchical world of *Nineteen Eighty-Four*:

> What is now arising is a new kind of planned, cen-tralised society which will be neither capitalist nor, in any accepted sense of the word, democratic. The rulers of this new society will be the people who effec-tively control the means of production: that is, busi-ness executives, technicians, bureaucrats, and soldiers, lumped together by Burnham under the name of

'managers'. These people will eliminate the old capitalist class, crush the working class, and so organise society that all power and economic privilege remain in their hands. Private property rights will be abolished, but common ownership will not be established. The new 'managerial' societies will not consist of a patchwork of small, independent states, but of great superstates grouped round the main industrial centres in Europe, Asia, and America. These super-states will fight among themselves for possession of the remaining uncaptured portions of the earth, but will probably be unable to conquer one another completely. Internally, each society will be hierarchical, with an aristocracy of talent at the top and a mass of semi-slaves at the bottom.

Oceania, with its tripartite structure of Inner Party, Outer Party, and proletariat, clearly owes something to Burnham's prophecies. Other journalism from the pre-Jura period shows Orwell exploring what might be called the psychology of totalitarianism and the intellectual deceits that have to be entered into in order for an autocratic society to function. An introduction to a volume of Jack London's short stories returns to *The Iron Heel* and notes that London foresaw 'that peculiar horror of totalitarian society, the way in which suspected enemies of the regime *simply disappear*'. Alternatively, in 'The Prevention of Literature', a long essay from January 1946, Orwell discusses 'the organised lying' practised by totalitarian states. This, Orwell argues, is not a temporary expedient but something integral to totalitarianism, 'something that would still continue even if concentration camps and secret police forces had ceased to be necessary'. To the autocrat, history's only importance is as a tool to maintain the power of the regime that manipulates it. Theoretically, the leaders of a totalitarian state are infallible, but in practice it is frequently necessary to rearrange certain events in order to present those leaders in a favourable light. Meanwhile, the frequent changes of doctrine and policy required to keep the regime afloat can only be explained away by a continual tampering with the record of past events. 'Totalitarianism demands, in fact, the continuous alteration of the past, and in the long run probably demands a disbelief in the very existence of objective truth'.

If these two essays are further evidence in Orwell's exposé of the totalitarian mind, then 'Politics and the English Language', published in *Horizon* in April 1946, examines the way in which the inflated style of modern political speech and writing is used to carry out these deceits. In a foretaste of the jargon phrases of Oceania's official news bulletins and the exhortatory clichés of its announcers, he notes that 'When there is a gap between one's real and one's declared aims, one turns, as it were instinctively to long words and exhausted idioms, like a cuttlefish squirting out ink'. 'Political language', he concludes, 'is designed to make lies sound truthful and murder respectable, and to give an appearance of solidity to pure wind'. The same point would shortly be made of Big Brother's speeches and the rewritten versions of *The Times* that Winston sits devising in his cubicle at the Ministry of Truth.

ORWELL SPENT the next six months in London, 'smothered under journalism' as he put it, brooding over the manuscript pages of *Nineteen Eighty-Four* and enduring one of the harshest winters in living memory—a key factor, he came to believe, in the slow deterioration of his health. Back on Jura in April 1947, he was determined to concentrate his energies on finishing the book. New commissions were waved away and friends who approached him with tempting proposals warned off. 'I am up here for 6 months trying to get on with a novel', he explained to a correspondent who had wondered what had happened to his *Tribune* column. 'I can't write anything now', he told George Woodcock, who seems to have suggested that he review a book in which they were both interested. 'I am struggling with this book of mine and trying not to do any journalism. I shan't finish the book by the end of the year, but I hope to break its back, which I shan't do if I undertake other jobs'. The difficulties he was experiencing in moulding his material into a suitable shape are a constant theme of his letters. 'I am struggling with this book which I *may* finish by the end of the year', he wrote to his agent, Leonard Moore, towards the end of May, adding that 'at any rate I shall have broken its back by then so long as I can keep well and keep off journalism work until the autumn'. The reference to 'keeping well' is significant. Orwell knew he was in poor shape and feared he would get worse. Time was pressing.

One of the most fascinating letters from the spring of 1947 was sent to the novel's prospective publisher, Fred Warburg. Nearly two years had passed since the internal memorandum noting that the first dozen pages were done. Keen to establish when it might be finished, Warburg had also been relieved to discover that Orwell had persuaded Victor Gollancz, to whom his next two novels were legally contracted, to give up his interest in the project ('I heard from Gollancz that he was willing to terminate the contract', Orwell had written to his agent in mid-April, 'so I suppose everything can be fixed up with Warburg'). Much of the letter to Warburg is simply an amplification of the notes written to friends in the previous six weeks. He has made 'a fairly good start' on the book, and thinks he 'must have written nearly a third of the rough draft'. If progress has been slower than anticipated it is 'because I have really been in most wretched health this year ever since January'. However, he keeps 'pegging away' and hopes to have finished the draft by the autumn. A possible completion date is set for early 1948, although Orwell adds the ominous proviso 'barring illnesses'. Significantly, he is now prepared to tell Warburg something about the book's contents. 'I don't like talking about books before they are written but I will tell you now that this is a novel about the future—that is, it is in a sense a fantasy, but in the form of a naturalistic novel. That is what makes it a difficult job'.

Even more fascinating, in the light of Nineteen Eighty-Four's final shape, is the paragraph that follows. Here Orwell notes that he is sending Warburg separately 'a long autobiographical sketch, which I originally undertook as a sort of pendant to Cyril Connolly's "Enemies of Promise", he having asked me to write a reminiscence of the preparatory school we were at together'. The sketch has not yet been sent to Horizon, Orwell explains, 'because apart from being too long for a periodical I think it is really too libellous to print, and I am not disposed to change it, except perhaps the names'. This is Orwell's first mention of 'Such, Such Were the Joys', a pitiless 15,000-word account of the five years (1911–16) he spent at St Cyprian's near Eastbourne on the Sussex coast. A high-profile prep school, adept at supplying scholarship-winning pupils to the major English public schools, St Cyprian's was owned and administered by a married couple named Wilkes whom the boys nicknamed 'Sambo' and 'Flip'. Such is the bitterness that Orwell brought to the record of the time he spent in their care—among other failings, the Wilkeses are accused of cruelty, snobbery, favouritism, and taking pleasure in humiliating their charges—that the essay could not be published until after his death, and even then, only in America: UK publication was delayed until as late as 1968.

No modern reader who examines 'Such, Such Were the Joys' alongside *Nineteen Eighty-Four* can fail to be struck by the similarities in their psychological atmosphere—a connection that becomes all the more startling when you recall that the one is set in a pre–Great War English boarding school and the other in a dystopian horror world where the citizenry amuse themselves by watching public executions. But there is no getting away from the fact that St Cyprian's, as reimagined by Orwell, is essentially a police state or that the young Eric Blair, sneered at by his teachers for his parents' lack of money and constantly being told that he will never amount to anything, is an early version of Winston Smith. At one point, for example, Orwell describes his younger self as feeling 'a sense of desperate loneliness and helplessness, of being locked up not only in a hostile world but in a world of good and evil where the rules were such that it was actually not possible for me to keep them'. Elsewhere he records the desolating sense of being constantly under surveillance, his every movement invigilated or monitored by all-seeing eyes. When he makes an illicit trip to a sweet shop and sees a passer-by staring fixedly at his school cap, there can be no doubt who the man is. 'He was a spy placed there by Sambo'. It did not seem strange to the 10-year-old boy that the headmaster of a private school should have an army of informers at his disposal, for 'Sambo was all-powerful and it was natural that his agents should be everywhere'.

Curiously, the man whom Mr Wilkes most obviously resembles is O'Brien, as he stands interrogating Winston in the Ministry of Love. If there is something almost priestly about O'Brien as he lectures Winston on the ultimate aim of the totalitarian project—not merely to tell a man that 2 + 2 = 5 but to induce him actually to believe it—then there is also something schoolmasterly about him, the sense of a patient, if sometimes exasperated pedagogue determined to take pains with a backward pupil in the hope that in the end he can be goaded into 'making good'. Orwell even notes that at one point in Winston's interrogation O'Brien 'assumed again his air of a schoolmaster questioning a promising pupil'. All this is uncomfortably close to Mr Wilkes catechising his charges over the date of the Battle of Waterloo. So, too, is Winston's psychological relationship with his tormentor. Winston despises O'Brien, but there is also a way in which he wishes to please him, come up with the answers that will satisfy him, deflect the torrent of accusation and reproach. In the same way, the young Eric is represented as loathing Sambo and Flip 'with a sort of shamefaced remorseful hatred'. All the boys hate and fear Flip, yet they 'all fawned on her in the most abject way, and the top layer of our feelings towards her was a sort of guilt-stricken loyalty'. Orwell remarks that he would be brought to the brink of tears by her exhortations to 'buck up' and behave better. 'And yet all the while, at the middle of one's heart, there seemed to stand an incorruptible inner self who knew that whatever one did—whether one laughed or snivelled or went into frenzies of gratitude for small favours—one's only true feeling was hatred'. And so like Oceania, St Cyprian's is a totalitarian regime, run by capricious tyrants whose word is law and where the rules are constantly being changed to the bewilderment of those being ruled. Significantly, Orwell claims that, like Winston Smith, his younger self learned 'that one can do wrong without ever discovering what one has done or why it was wrong'.

The precise relation of 'Such, Such Were the Joys' to *Nineteen Eighty-Four* rests on the date of its composition. Sadly, this is impossible to prove. Once he returned to Jura, Orwell had begun to send batches of the novel to a typist, Mrs Miranda Christen, to whom he had sublet the Islington flat. Mrs Christen remembered producing a fair copy of the essay early in 1947, but she also recalled that the typescript from which she worked was clearly showing its age and might have been several years old. Confusingly, the surviving manuscript looks as if it was typed by three separate people. One of them was Mrs Christen. Another was Orwell himself, using his Barnhill typewriter. But the middle section, though produced on the Barnhill machine, is the work of someone else, possibly a summer visitor. None of this tells us when Orwell began work on it. *Horizon*, for which it was originally intended, began life at the end of 1939; Orwell started writing for it in the following year. A letter survives from 1938 in which he announces his intention of 'writing a book about St Cyprian's'. A likely outline of the essay's conception is that a first draft was completed in the early years of the war, that it was revised and retyped commercially in 1945–6, taken to Jura and then retyped by Mrs Christen in 1947 before being reworked for a third time.

But however, and whenever, it was written, one thing is certain: 'Such, Such Were the Joys' was vitally important to Orwell, an essay to which he was prepared to devote considerable amounts of his time, several times revised and restructured, and which he was eager to see between hard covers ('I think it should be printed sooner or later when the people most concerned are dead', he told Warburg, 'and maybe sooner or later I might do a book of collected sketches'). Why else would he have spent time tinkering with it on Jura when, as he assured half a dozen of his correspondents, he was worried about his health and desperate to forge ahead with *Nineteen Eighty-Four*? And while it is impossible to demonstrate either that *Nineteen Eighty-Four* grew out of these projections of his youthful misery or that the essay itself is a by-product of the landscapes of Oceania, there is clearly some kind of relationship between the two. Both seem to have been forged out of the same materials: without 'Such, Such Were the Joys', it is fair to say, *Nineteen Eighty-Four* would have been a substantially different piece of work.

QUITE AS INTRIGUING as the correspondence with Fred Warburg is what seems to be the very first letter that Orwell despatched from Jura on the day after his arrival there. Three pages long, and containing minutely itemised instructions on how to reach the island from the Scottish mainland ('Travel by bus to West Tarbert . . . Take hired car to Lealt'), it was sent neither to his publisher nor a literary friend but to Sonia Brownell, the woman whom, thirty months later in a ceremony conducted in a London hospital room, he was to marry. Sonia, at this point in her career, was an assistant on *Horizon*, where she combined a profound reverence for Connolly's intellect with an undisguised desire to take on more of the editorial duties herself. She was also one of the women to whom, in the winter of 1945–6, Orwell had proposed marriage and by whom he had been turned down. A year later, their relationship had progressed to the point where Orwell is anxious to write to her even before his luggage has been unpacked ('Dearest Sonia, I am handwriting this because my typewriter is downstairs'), thank her for purchases made on his behalf ('I've just remembered I never paid you for that brandy you got for me'), and entreat her to visit him ('I want to give you the complete details about the journey, which isn't so formidable as it looks on paper'). Clearly the man who signs off 'with much love', having remarked that 'I do so want to have you here', is desperate to have her by his side.

Sonia never made it to Jura in Orwell's lifetime. Possibly she was put off by the prospect of a journey so torturous that it took Orwell two dozen lines to describe. Nonetheless, the memory of her, and the time they had spent together in London, would have been at the forefront of his mind as he sat down to recommence work on *Nineteen Eighty-Four* and sketch out the doomed love affair that lies at its core. All this, naturally, encourages a suspicion that Sonia bears some relation to Julia, the 'girl from the fiction department', who spends her working hours in a government department engaged on the task of mass-producing pornography for impressionable proles and her leisure hours encouraging Winston to break almost every proscription in the Party rule book. Hilary Spurling, in her portrait of Sonia, goes even further and declares that Orwell returned to Jura in the spring of 1947 with the aim of 'recreating' Sonia as Julia and a determination to 'take her as his model'. First catching sight of Julia as she enters a room in which the Two Minutes Hate is being staged, Winston sees a bold-looking girl of about twenty-seven, with thick dark hair, a freckled face and swift, athletic movements. A narrow scarlet sash, emblem of the Junior Anti-Sex League, was wound several times round the waist of her overalls, just tightly enough to bring out the shapeliness of her hips.

Julia's age is later given as 26 (Sonia, by the time Orwell invited her to Jura, was in sight of her twenty-ninth birthday), and several pointed distinctions are made between her youthful zest and Winston's premature decay ('I'm thirty-nine years old. I've got a wife I can't get rid of. I've got varicose veins. I've got five false teeth'). Orwell, at the time he first asked Sonia to marry him, was in his early forties. In both cases a distinctly unhealthy middle-aged man is obsessed with an energetic woman in her twenties. After this, though, evidence for the Sonia/Julia identification is much more ambiguous. Winston at one point notes of Julia that 'Except for her mouth, you could not call her beautiful'; Sonia, with her ash-blonde hair, pale complexion, and slight tendency to plumpness, was thought by her admirers to resemble a Renoir portrait. Like Sonia, Julia has a forceful presence, is said to 'burst' into rooms, and has a self-confident vocal style that approaches the bossiness Sonia was thought to bring to her editorial work duties in the *Horizon* office. Julia's declaration that 'I do voluntary work three evenings a week for the Junior Anti-Sex League. Hours and hours I've spent pasting their bloody rot all over London. I always carry one end of the banner in the processions. I always look cheerful and I never shirk anything' sounds very like some of Sonia's quoted remarks. Unlike her supposed model, Julia is resolutely unintellectual, doesn't care much for reading—to

Sonia, a friend once recalled, 'man could do nothing greater than to write books'—and falls asleep while Winston regales her with selections from Oceania's legendary banned book, Emmanuel Goldstein's *The Theory and Practice of Oligarchical Collectivism*.

But there are other pieces of evidence, from both *Nineteen Eighty-Four* and the circumstances of Orwell's life, which might call the identification into question. To begin with, Orwell had started thinking about the novel well before he became involved with Sonia in the early part of 1946. The *plein-air* frolics that Winston enjoys with Julia are prefigured as early as Orwell's relationship with Eleanor Jaques, most of which was conducted in the Suffolk countryside in the early 1930s. A letter to Eleanor from September 1932, which recalls 'that day in the wood along past Blythburgh Lodge . . . I shall always remember that, & your nice white body in the dark moss', is remarkably close to the account of Julia tearing off her clothes so that her body 'gleamed white in the sun'. As for Julia's 'swift, athletic movements', it is worth pointing out that Brenda Salkeld, another of Orwell's Suffolk loves from the early 1930s, held down a day job as gym mistress at a local girls' private school.

A third objection is perhaps more integral to the role that Julia plays in the book, which is to a certain extent figurative rather than decisive. Curiously, with the exception of Winston's opening remarks and one or two speculations about her interior life ('She was very young, he thought, she still expected something from life . . . She would not accept it as a law of nature that the individual is always defeated . . . She did not understand that there was no such thing as happiness, that the only victory lay in the far future, long after you were dead'), we learn very little about Julia, and what goes on in her mind. Winston, with the memory of his miserable, sex-loathing wife to goad him, may find Julia irresistible, but there is a way in which her importance rests on what she symbolises—youth, impulse, free-spiritedness—rather than what she actually is.

But to Spurling, Sonia is not merely transposed onto the pages of *Nineteen Eighty-Four*, she is also a significant influence on its intellectual framework. One of the key concepts of Oceania's totalitarian regime is the state of mind encapsulated by the Newspeak word 'doublethink'—the ability to hold simultaneously in your head two contradictory opinions. There are certainly echoes, or rather foreshadowings, of doublethink in a review Sonia contributed to *Horizon* in July 1946 of *Les Amitiés particulières* by the French writer Roger Peyrefitte. Like the two boys who are its central characters, Sonia had been educated at a Catholic boarding school, and the book reawakened many a hostile memory of the atmosphere of treachery and duplicitousness which she imagined to lie at Catholicism's heart:

> When you have seen through [this] world you can never become its victim, but can fight it with the only unanswerable weapon—cynical despair; when you have learned the lesson of the double visions, action and emotion are equally meaningless. This is the heritage of Catholic education . . . one which those who went to Catholic schools always recognise in each other, members of a secret society who, when they meet, huddle together, temporarily at truce with the rest of the world, while they, cautiously, untrustingly, lick each other's wounds.

It is not known whether this particular issue of *Horizon* reached Jura in the summer of 1946, but Spurling thinks it 'hard to write off as coincidence the fact that, at the very moment when he started work on *Nineteen Eighty-Four*, his ex-mistress outlined in print precisely the scenario that would become the central section of his plot'. On the other hand, a trawl through Orwell's journalism suggests that he had been attempting to equate religious faith with left- and right-wing forms of autocracy throughout the early 1940s. There is, for example, an unpublished review originally filed for the *Manchester Evening News*—as with *Animal Farm*, Orwell assumed that it was rejected for its 'anti-Stalin implications'—of Harold Laski's *Faith, Reason and Civilisation*. Laski's aim was to square his belief in democracy and freedom of thought with his conviction that the Soviet Union is 'the real dynamo of the Socialist movement in this country and everywhere else'. According to Orwell's reading, Laski does this by drawing an analogy between the USSR and Christianity in the period of the break-up of the Roman Empire; Soviet socialism 'aims at the establishment of human brotherhood and equality just as single-mindedly as the early church aimed at the establishment of the Kingdom of God'.

Certainly, there are traces of Sonia in *Nineteen Eighty-Four*, just as there are hints of Orwell's first wife Eileen, who in her late twenties contributed a three-part futurist satire entitled 'End of the Century: 1984' to her old school magazine, which Orwell is highly likely to have seen. Meanwhile, there is a final reason for wondering whether the girl in the fiction department is a straightforward projection of the girl who fussed over Cyril Connolly in the *Horizon* office. This is the question of Julia's motivation, and the ultimate value of her feelings for Winston. For O'Brien, the potentate of the Inner Party, the sacerdotal, schoolmasterly figure who encourages Winston in his rebellion, is eventually revealed as an agent provocateur; the plot is a put-up job; there is at least a suspicion that Julia is O'Brien's willing accomplice, the honeytrap expressly set in place with the aim of luring Winston into danger and throwing him into the hands of the Thought Police. *Nineteen Eighty-Four* may well, from one angle, be a love letter from Jura to a girl left behind in London. From another, its central message would seem to be that in the end the people we love are guaranteed to betray us.

HUNKERED DOWN ON JURA, as the wind tore in from the Atlantic and the cormorants massed in the bay, Orwell began to keep another 'domestic diary' of his exploits on the island. Taken up whenever *Nineteen Eighty-Four* was put down, and mostly concerned with the flora and fauna of Barnhill ('Some hens moulting. Today a double egg, supposed to be a bad sign, as it is said to be the last of the clutch'), the journal has several points of connection with the novel running alongside it. Not only is it a reliable guide to Orwell's declining health, but in amid the nature notes there are occasional hints of the way in which Jura was capable of stirring his creative imagination. In the first category are some parenthetic entries from the first few weeks of his stay which suggest that he was sufficiently ill to be confined to the house ('*Still not feeling well enough to do much out of doors*', 22 April. '*Not feeling well enough to do much*'. 9 May. '*Better. Went out a little but did not do anything*'. 13 May). In the second is a

note that directly relates to an incident halfway through Part II
of the novel. Winston and Julia have just woken up in their eyrie
above Mr Charrington's shop when she lets out a cry of 'Hi! Get
out, you filthy brute!'

> She suddenly twisted herself over in the bed, seized a
> shoe from the floor, and sent it hurling into the cor-
> ner with a boyish jerk of her arm, exactly as he had
> seen her fling the dictionary at Goldstein that morning
> during the Two Minutes Hate.
> 'What was it?' he said in surprise.
> 'A rat. I saw him stick his beastly nose out of the
> wainscoting. There's a hole down there. I gave him a
> good fright, anyway'.
> 'Rats!' murmured Winston. 'In this room'.
> 'They're all over the place', said Julia indiffer-
> ently as she lay down again. 'We've even got them in
> the kitchen at the hostel. Some parts of London are
> swarming with them. Did you know they attack chil-
> dren? Yes, they do. In some streets a woman daren't
> leave her baby alone for two minutes. It's the great huge
> brown ones that do it. And the nasty thing is that the
> brutes always—'
> '*Don't go on!*' said Winston, with his eyes
> tightly shut.

The 'nasty thing' that the brutes always do can be traced to a diary
entry from 12 June in which a paragraph about the surprising
ease with which the Barnhill rats allow themselves to be caught

in the traps set in the byre ends with a piece of news from one of the nearby villages: '*I hear that recently two children at Ardlussa were bitten by rats (in the face, as usual.)*'

The friends who visited Orwell on Jura in the spring and summer of 1947 were convinced that he was happy there, quietly adapting himself to a routine of work about the farm, amusing the three-year-old Richard, occasional trips to nearby rivers in search of trout, gleefully extirpating the area's snake population, and trying to hatch frogspawn in a jar. Although the novel sel-dom flowed smoothly, he believed that he was making progress. 'My book is getting on very slowly', he told George Woodcock in the second week of June, 'but still it is getting on. I hope to finish it fairly early in 1948'. A similar report was sent to Leonard Moore, at the end of July: 'I am getting on fairly well with the novel and expect to finish the rough draft by October. I dare say it will take me another six months after that'. If the finishing line still seemed some way off, it was because Orwell was uncertain of his whereabouts over the winter. Mindful of what the freeze-up of 1946–7 had done to his lungs, he wondered whether it might not be better to pay a short visit to London in the autumn and then return to Jura, where the weather seemed more temperate and fuel was in plentiful supply. A letter to Warburg written on the first day of September reports that he expects to be in London 'roughly for November' and not before that date 'unless some-thing unexpected happens'. As for the novel, he hopes to finish the rough draft sometime in October and expects the rewriting to occupy him for four or five months. 'It is an awful mess at present', Orwell helpfully concludes, 'but I think has possibilities'.

But by this time Orwell had already been involved in an inci-dent which very nearly brought his work on *Nineteen Eighty-Four* to a dead stop. Two weeks before, he and Richard, accompanied by Avril and three of Barnhill's summer visitors, his nieces Jane and Lucy Dakin and their brother Henry, had set off by boat to make the ninety-minute journey to a camping site at Glengarrisdale. Avril and Jane decided to walk back across the island to Barnhill. Returning by sea, and having misread the tide tables, Orwell and his passengers ended up in the famous Corryvreckan whirlpool, lost their engine—this sheared away from its mounting and vanished into the sea—and endured a dangerous moment when their boat turned over and came to rest on a rocky outcrop a mile from the Jura coast. They were eventually rescued by a passing lobster boat, but the effect on Orwell's health of his immersion in the Atlantic Ocean and the five-mile walk back to Barnhill from the spot where the rescue boat had dropped them was apparent within a couple of weeks. *'Felt unwell, did nothing out of doors'* runs a diary entry from early September. Two days later Orwell notes that he is *'Unwell (chest), hardly went outside'*. There were late-September fishing trips and work about the farm, but the entry for 13 October is an ominous *'Unwell, did not go out'*.

Upstairs in the study bedroom, the manuscript pages were stacking up; the first draft was nearly done. But there were to be no trips to London, and the lecture Orwell had intended to give at the Working Men's College in Camden Town was eventually cancelled. In nearly every letter he wrote over the next two months the tocsin of his bad health clangs relentlessly away. 'I have been in wretched health a lot of the year—my chest as usual', he told Arthur Koestler. As late as the fourth week in October he was still intending to travel south and reporting to Woodcock that the draft was virtually complete ('I haven't got on as fast as I should because I've been in such wretched health this year') but by the last day of the month he was confined to bed, with what he told his agent was 'inflammation of the lungs'. Thereafter the bulletins sent to friends and professional associates grew steadily worse. 'I have been very unwell & intend to stay in bed for some weeks & try & get right again', he told his agent early in November. A letter to Koestler talks about needing to 'see a specialist', and the probability of having to stay in a nursing home ('I've really been very bad for several months tho' I didn't take to my bed until about 3 weeks ago'), while a note sent to a journalist on the *Observer* represents him as 'merely trying to get well enough to make the journey to London & see a specialist'. As for *Nineteen Eighty-Four*, 'I am just halfway through a book which I am supposed to finish in the spring or early summer, but which of course I can't touch till I'm well enough'.

'I think I am now really getting better', he told Moore on the last day of November, but the rest of the letter sets the gravity of his situation in sharp relief. There is a chest specialist coming to see him from Glasgow in the following week. Whatever his ability to leave Jura, 'I am bound to be incapacitated for some time, & I dare say after that they will tell me to go to a hot climate for a month or two'. He has done no work on the novel for over a month, and there is still four or five months needed to complete it. Meanwhile, his American publishers should have it impressed on them that 'I am & have been seriously ill'. The chest specialist, arriving from the mainland in the first week of December, confirmed what Orwell had long supposed: 'as I feared, I am seriously ill', he told Moore. 'It's T.B., as I suspected. They think they can cure it all right, but I am bound to be hors de combat for a good while'. The specialist had recommended that he go into a sanatorium near Glasgow, he told his friend Celia Kirwan, 'for about 4 months. It's an awful bore, however perhaps it's all for the best if they can cure me'. Shortly before Christmas he was taken to Hairmyres Hospital in East Kilbride, where a consultant diagnosed 'chronic' tuberculosis, consisting of a largish cavity in his left lung and a smaller patch at the top of the right.

Looming over this chronicle of dissolution (among other symptoms, Orwell had lost nearly 10 kg in weight) hangs the question of delay. Friends who had stayed on Jura in the spring and summer of 1947 had noticed how frail he was looking. He had spent much of his eight months on the island as a semi-invalid. Why had he had taken so long to get himself properly treated? The answer lies in the pile of paper lying in the study bedroom at Barnhill. As Orwell explained to his friend Julian Symons shortly after his arrival at Hairmyres:

> I thought early in the year I was seriously ill but rather foolishly decided to stave it off for a year as I'd just started writing a book. Of course what happened was that I half finished the book, which is much the same as not starting it, & then was so ill I had to take to my bed . . . With luck I'll be all right by the summer. They seem confident of being able to patch me up.

Throughout his life, Orwell had always underplayed his health problems. But the breezy tone of the letter to Symons, with its talk about the doctors' confidence in being able to patch him up, masks a private trauma. Lying in bed at Barnhill as the bleak December days faded into dusk, he had several long conversations with his landlord, and fellow Old Etonian, Robin Fletcher. Although Fletcher was some years younger than his tenant, the two men got on well. No precise record exists of what was said between them, but Fletcher was sure, as he put it to his wife Margaret, that Orwell *knew*. The only thing he wanted from however much of his life remained to him was to finish his novel while there was still time.

ORWELL SPENT seven months at Hairmyres. Here he underwent a painful procedure that involved repeatedly collapsing his left lung and then refilling it with air, was force-fed to increase his weight ('They make me eat a tremendous lot', he reported), and treated with streptomycin, the new wonder drug from America whose novelty was such that none of the medical professionals who administered it had any idea of the correct dosage. Always stoical in the face of physical inconvenience, Orwell noted that the side effects included his hair falling out, his fingernails disintegrating, and ulcerated blisters in his throat. Nevertheless, he believed that he was slowly getting better. As early as the third week in January he was able to tell Celia that 'today when I was X-rayed the doctor said he could see definite improvement'. By early April he had put on 1.5 kg and recorded that three successive sputum tests had come back negative. Not long afterwards he was allowed out of bed for a short time during the day, and by the end of May, though 'frightfully weak & thin' and short of breath, he was able to take brief walks around the hospital grounds. It was a nice hospital, he told well-wishers, '& everyone is very kind to me'.

Meanwhile, he was brooding about his book and his inability to finish it. 'I can't do any serious work', he told Julian Symons, shortly after his arrival. 'I never can in bed, even when I feel well. I can't show you the part-finished novel. I never show them to anybody, because they are just a mess & don't have much relationship to the final draft. I always say a book doesn't exist until it is finished'. Writing to Warburg, a month later, he explained that the first draft was complete except for 'the last few hundred words'. As for future plans:

> If I'm well & out of here by June, I might just finish it by the end of the year—I don't know. It is just a ghastly mess as it stands, but the idea is so good that I could not possibly abandon it. If anything should happen to me I've instructed Richard Rees, my literary executor, to destroy the MS without showing it to anybody, but it's unlikely that anything like that would happen. This disease isn't dangerous at my age, & they say the cure is going on quite well, though slowly.

Though characteristically underplayed and self-deprecating, this is a revealing letter: Orwell knows he is onto something with *Nineteen Eighty-Four*, pines to see it through, and wants it to be perfect—so much so that he is prepared to see it destroyed rather than published incomplete. And all the while, lurking in the background, is the fear that death or incapacity may intervene. There was a certain amount to interest him as he slowly recuperated— news of his son's progress, occasional book reviews for the *Observer* and the *Manchester Evening News*, Secker & Warburg's plans for a uniform edition of his works—but, as he complained to Celia Kirwan, it was 'sad' to be reprinting old books rather than getting on with a new one. If the enforced idleness had done him good, then he was also 'getting a bit fed up with lying in bed, now that spring is starting, & longing to get home & go fishing'.

As spring turned into summer, the urge to return to the novel became irresistible. He had started revising, he told Warburg's partner Roger Senhouse in mid-May, but was only able to do a very little, 'perhaps an hour's work each day'. By this stage, the question of what might happen to him after his discharge was in the air: one idea was that he might have to continue treatment as an outpatient. A fortnight later he reported himself as being 'ever so much better & for some time past they have not been able to find any germs in me'. After repeated tests had proved negative, the Hairmyres doctors decided that he could return to Barnhill at the end of July. 'Of course I have got to go on living a semi-invalid life for a long time, perhaps as long as a year', he told Moore, 'but I don't mind as I have got quite used to working in bed'. Warburg, who had heard of the improvement in Orwell's health and been kept abreast of his letter to Senhouse, decided that the moment had come for a little exhortation. He was 'of course specially pleased' to hear about the revision, he wrote in mid-July, for this was 'far and away the most single undertaking to which you could apply yourself when the vitality is there'. What Warburg had heard about the novel had convinced him that this could be a publishing sensation. But it was crucial that the author of this bestseller in embryo should not be distracted from the things that mattered most. 'It should not be put aside for reviews or miscellaneous work, however tempting, and will I am certain bring in more money than you could expect from any other activity'. If Orwell could finish his revisions by the end of the year this would be 'pretty satisfactory', as Secker could publish in autumn 1949. 'But it really is rather important from the point of view of your literary career to get it done by the end of the year, and indeed earlier if at all possible', Warburg entreated. A day or so later, with these blandishments ringing in his ears, Orwell returned to Jura.

INEVITABLY, much of what Orwell's friends wrote about his behaviour in the last eighteen months of his life is coloured by melodramatic hindsight. In the second volume of his memoirs, for example, published over twenty years after he first set eyes on the manuscript of *Nineteen Eighty-Four*, Warburg writes that 'Jura was where Orwell wanted to be, his Mecca, where the loner could be alone, where he could wrestle with the creation of *1984* and with the Angel of Death'. Did Orwell really think he was dying? And what effect did this have on his writing? The Hairmyres medical staff who discharged him in the summer of 1948 thought he was better: the TB bacilli had disappeared from his lungs. Friends on Jura, remembering the emaciated spectre who had left the island seven months before, marked the improvement in his health. None of this, though, meant that Orwell was destined to recover. The fibrotic tuberculosis from which he had been suffering had left the arteries in his lungs dangerously exposed. Great care had to be taken—a quiet, restorative convalescence, ideally involving long hours of bed rest and an avoidance of stress and upset. Naturally, Orwell being Orwell, these were precisely the things he was determined to deny himself.

Barnhill was full of visitors: friends come for the summer or to help with the Jura harvest. At one point there were so many people staying that tents had to be pitched in the garden.

Cautioned by his doctors to avoid physical activity, Orwell settled down to a sedentary existence spent mostly in his bedroom. 'I only get up for half a day', he explained to Moore, 'and can't manage any kind of exertion'. But he felt 'much better', he assured his friends. Unless he became ill again 'or something of that kind', the novel would be finished by December. In early September, Warburg was informed that Orwell was 'about half-way through the revisions' and that his health was holding up. Then in early autumn something went wrong. '*Very unwell, temperature above 100 each evening*' runs a diary note from mid-September. '*Unwell, stayed in bed*', he wrote on 8 October. Five days later there is an ominous '*Pain in side very bad on & off*'.

The immediate cause of the relapse seems to have been a return visit to Glasgow to be X-rayed by the Hairmyres specialists. Certainly, Orwell told David Astor that although Mr Dick, the senior doctor who oversaw his treatment, was pleased with the results of the examination, 'the journey upset me'. Thereafter, the diary entries turn grimmer by the day: '*Pain in side very bad on & off*' (16 October); '*Felt very bad in afternoon & evening, no doubt as a result of going out*' (6 November). Although, characteristically, Orwell played down quite how wretched he was feeling, the letters he wrote to friends in London make plain just how rapidly his condition had worsened. He could work, he explained, but that was about all he could do. Even to walk half a mile upset him, he told Julian Symons at the end of October. To Anthony Powell, a fortnight later, he complained that he could not so much as 'pull up a weed in the garden'. Already there was talk of wintering out in a sanatorium on the mainland, or even leaving the UK altogether. 'I could go abroad perhaps', he hazarded to Symons, 'but the journey might be the death of me'.

In these circumstances, the urge to finish the book grew yet more compelling and, at the same time, ever more frustrating. Desperate to complete the revisions, Orwell seems to have been afraid that he was letting himself down, rushing at work that needed time and reflection. It was awful to think he had been 'mucking about with this book since June 1947', he lamented to Powell, 'and it's a ghastly mess now, a good idea ruined, but of course I was seriously ill for 7 or 8 months of the time'. He was seriously ill now, but determined to send the manuscript to Warburg before he became worse. It was almost done, he told Moore towards the end of October, while a letter to Warburg written on the same day maintains that 'I shall finish the book D.V. [*Deo volente*—i.e. 'God willing'] early in November, and I am rather flinching from the job of typing it, because it is a very awkward thing to do in bed, where I still have to spend half the time'. As for a judgement on the contents:

> I am not pleased with the book but I am not absolutely dissatisfied ... I think it is a good idea but the execution would have been better if I had not written it under the influence of TB. I haven't definitely fixed on the title but I am hesitating between NINETEEN EIGHTY-FOUR and THE LAST MAN IN EUROPE.

Sometime in early November, looking out at the grey Jura skies where the sea eagles and buzzards that always fascinated him wheeled back and forth, he made up his mind. It would be *Nineteen Eighty-Four*. But the letter to Warburg canvasses a problem that, it is fair to say, shortened Orwell's life. On the day he sent it he also despatched a telegram with the urgent request: could

Warburg find him a secretary who would be prepared to travel to Jura and, under his supervision, retype the manuscript? As he explained to Moore, a week later, it was 'a tiresome job when one is too weak to sit up at a table for long periods, and in any case can't be done in bed, where I have to be half the day'. On the other hand, it couldn't be sent away 'because it is in too much of a mess to be intelligible unless I was there to decipher it'. Could Moore help? For a fortnight, efforts were made to find a typist who would be prepared to travel from either London or the Scottish mainland, spend what was estimated at a fortnight on Jura, and endure two sea voyages and a great deal of incidental inconvenience as part of the bargain. Roger Senhouse applied to his niece, then living in Scotland ('an efficient girl who knows most people in Edinburgh, or at any rate how to get hold of the right person for the purpose in hand'). Moore produced two possible candidates, but hesitated to close the deal while the efficient girl went about her work. In the end, there were no takers: Orwell, as he reported to Powell in mid-November, decided to undertake the 'grisly job' himself.

Short of running around the Barnhill garden, there was no activity more likely calculated to worsen Orwell's health than the one on which he now embarked: propped up in bed, warmed by the glare of a defective paraffin heater, and chain-smoking his hand-rolled cigarettes while, hunched over a rickety typewriter, he made a fair copy plus two carboned facsimiles of a much scrawled-over manuscript. The job could have waited until the spring. Why was he determined to finish it at the expense of his ravaged lungs? More than one critic, horrified by the ordeal that he put himself through to complete *Nineteen Eighty-Four*, has advertised the theory of Orwell's 'fatalism', or—a variation on this—the idea that, as his publisher once put it, 'he might have killed himself by gross negligence'. Warburg's account of the last months of 1948 carries a shrewd analysis of his star author's motives. Orwell, he pronounced, was a stoic. 'What he considered tolerable would have been felt to be quite intolerable by many'. Sonia Brownell, when asked by one of Orwell's friends why he did not simply come south for the winter with his typescript and avail himself of professional help, made the same point:

> Oh, George was perfectly aware that he could come to London and engage an efficient secretary, but as he saw things, leaving Jura was just not on. It would have meant an upheaval in his whole consciousness of himself, which he did not want to face. Besides, all his life he had ignored his illnesses up to the point where they got too bad, when he went to bed and waited to recover as he always did.

The bed-bound month hunched over the typewriter while the Atlantic winds beat at the window was less an unconscious attempt to kill himself than a classic example of how Orwell behaved, what Warburg and Sonia Brownell diagnose as his failure to recognise the need for precautions and his dislike of having to behave like an invalid. The relapse that followed his return trip to Hairmyres was, according to Warburg, merely the result of Orwell not taking sufficient care of himself—in this case omitting to reserve a room at a time when all the Glasgow hotels were full and having to traipse from one venue to another carrying a heavy bag.

And so the task ground on. The typing was nearly half-finished. Orwell would let him have the completed job early in

December, he told Warburg on 22 November. Six days later he wrote to his sister-in-law, Gwen O'Shaughnessy, asking her to recommend a sanatorium where he might stay for the worst of the winter. By now the typing was almost finished. A typically self-deprecating letter to Moore worries that the typing agencies his agent had applied to had been put to unnecessary trouble and suggests that 'it really wasn't worth all this fuss'. Then, on 4 December, he breasted the finishing tape. 'I have sent off two copies of the MS of my book to you and one to Warburg', he told Moore, adding the diffident sign-off 'Perhaps you could acknowledge them when received, because there is always a slight possibility of a mishap in the post'. The domestic diary for 7 December mentions a little rain in the morning, a calm sea, Avril bringing back chunks of fat from the butcher after the slaughtering of the Barnhill pig, and finally, the fact that the writer is *'Feeling very unwell'*.

In fact, he was in a state of complete physical collapse, confined to bed and awaiting news from the sanatoria recommended by Gwen. The likeliest destination was Cranham in Gloucestershire, he told his friend Tosco Fyvel. ('E is still far from well & is going to take some more treatment in Jan & Feb', an equally stoical Avril informed her brother-in-law, adding that 'he has just finished his book which he has been working at for the last eighteen months, so I think that is a relief to his mind'). By now the consequences of the typing stint had begun to sink in. 'I am really very ill', he admitted to Fyvel. He should have headed south two months before, 'but I simply had to finish the book I am writing'. Still he was worried about book reviews he had promised to file ('The latter I will do & send off in the next few days', he told David Astor, 'but the other I just can't in my present state'). He acknowledged that 'I feel I simply must stop working, or rather trying to work, for a month or two'. The final diary entry dates from Christmas Eve ('*Snowdrops up all over the place. A few tulips showing. Some wallflowers still trying to flower*'). Early in the New Year, escorted by Richard Rees, he went south by train. Several hundred miles away, the manuscript of *Nineteen Eighty-Four* lay on Warburg's desk. Whatever might now befall Orwell, the job was done.

6. THE LAST MAN IN EUROPE

DOWN IN LONDON the novel had acquired its first readers. 'This is among the most terrifying books I have ever read', an awestruck Fred Warburg proclaimed in an elaborate in-house memorandum of 13 December 1948: in debt to the Jack London of *The Iron Heel*, perhaps, 'but in verisimilitude and horror he surpasses this not inconsiderable author'. Like many students of the rapidly evolving Cold War, Warburg assumed that *Nineteen Eighty-Four* had a single target with profound implications for his domestic audience: 'Here is the Soviet Union to the nth degree, a Stalin who never dies, a secret police with every device of modern technology'. Warburg suggested that 'it might well be described as a horror novel, and would make a horror film which, if licensed, might secure all countries threatened by communism for 1000 years to come'. Then there was the fact that Ingsoc, Oceania's ideological underpinning, was clearly a truncation of 'English Socialism'. As such, he was mindful of the propagandist uses to which the novel might be put. 'It seems to indicate a final breach between Orwell and socialism, not the socialism of equality and human brotherhood which Orwell clearly no longer expects of socialist parties but the socialism of Marxism and the managerial revolution . . . and it is worth a cool million votes to the Conservative party'. A Conservative Party, more to the point, whose leader, Winston Smith, shared the hero's Christian name.

Quite apart from its shocked enthusiasm for the novel ('It is a great book, but I pray I may be spared from reading another like it for years to come'), there are several intriguing subtexts to Warburg's precis. The first is its assumption that *Nineteen Eighty-Four* is the second instalment of what will ultimately develop into a trilogy, a kind of anthropomorphic version of *Animal Farm*, with the prospect of a third novel which will 'supply the other side of the picture'. The second is its canvassing of the idea that Orwell's illness had, in however indirect a way, affected his mental state. Winston's encounters with O'Brien ('his Grand Inquisitor') reminded Warburg of Dostoevsky: 'I cannot but think that this book could have been written only by a man who, however temporarily, had lost hope, and for physical reasons which are sufficiently apparent'. Turning to the book's commercial prospects, Warburg insisted that it should be published as soon as possible, ideally in June 1949. David Farrar, an associate to whom he had passed the manuscript, was equally enthusiastic. Orwell had done something that H.G. Wells had never managed to bring off, he declared, which was to create a fantasy world so real that the reader *minded* what happened to the characters. Bestseller-dom beckoned, together with critical acclaim ('We obviously can't print 50,000 copies, but I think we ought in the next month or so to consider whether 15,000 ought not to be a minimum printing'). Both men agreed that, as Farrar put it, the novel 'towers above the average'. All that was needed was to bring it to an expectant public.

Orwell accepted these compliments with his usual diffidence. A letter acknowledging Warburg's torrent of praise, written while he lay in bed at Barnhill, waits until the third paragraph before remarking that he is glad his publisher enjoyed the novel, while suggesting that 'it isn't a book I would gamble on for a big sale'. As ever with Orwell in the last few years of his life, and for all the fatalism sometimes attributed to him by friends, it is impossible to establish quite what state he believed himself to be in or how he imagined the future would pan out. The same letter, though acknowledging his complete physical prostration and the need for rest, also reveals his restlessness. Even now, with a year and a half's hard work behind him and his health irretrievably broken down, his mind was already moving on to the next project ('I am trying to finish off my scraps of book-reviewing etc. & must then just strike work for a month or so. I can't go on at present. I have a stunning idea for a short novel which has been in my head for years, but I can't start anything until I am free from high temperatures etc.'). Did Orwell really believe that a month's furlough would see him through? Or was he simply refusing to contemplate the seriousness of his situation?

Whatever the answer, the context in which the book moved towards publication was unignorable. This was a publishing process largely administered—at any rate from the author's side—from a hospital bed, where proof sheets lay scattered alongside temperature charts, editorial conferences were conducted by letter rather than telephone or visits to Secker's London office, and there could be no question of interviews and personal appearances to promote the book. To give only a single example of the circumventing of normal publishing practice demanded by Orwell's illness: one of the artefacts stored in the Orwell Archive is a small jewellery box. Inside are several scraps of paper bearing Orwell's signature. The assumption is that these were intended for presentation copies of the novel. Of all Orwell's works, autographed copies of *Nineteen Eighty-Four* are the rarest, if only because the author—bed bound and at this point confined to a Cotswold sanatorium—was unable to sign more than a handful of them.

Cranham, at which Orwell arrived in the first week of January 1949, lay high in the Gloucestershire hills, remote and difficult to access by either car or public transport. Anthony Powell and Malcolm Muggeridge, who opted to walk from the nearest railway station, found themselves faced with an eighteen-mile round trip. The patient, all those who saw him agreed, was in a desperate state. 'I hope the poor fellow will do well', Bruce Dick, his consultant at Hairmyres, had told David Astor. 'It is now obvious that he will need to live a most sheltered life in a sanatorium environment. I fear the dream of Jura must fade'. Tosco Fyvel and his wife, who visited Orwell early in the New Year, thought him 'terribly emaciated, his face drawn and waxen pallor'. The Warburgs, who followed them, were aghast at what they found. 'I don't think he'll live more than a year', Pamela Warburg told her husband as they set off back to London. The sanatorium itself seemed a grim place: the patients quartered in wooden huts; the conditions spartan; the medical regime far from intensive. The Warburgs discovered that, two weeks into his stay, Orwell had yet to see the chief physician or have a stethoscope applied to his chest: he supposed, he told anxious friends, that the doctors knew what they were doing.

Meanwhile, *Nineteen Eighty-Four* was hurtling towards publication. Warburg had taken soundings in the UK book trade: almost every comment that came back to him confirmed his hunch that the novel would be a roaring success. 'I knew it would sell', Muggeridge confided to his diary. Mondadori had already bought the Italian translation rights. Orwell's American publishers, Harcourt, Brace and Company, shared Warburg's enthusiasm ('one of the most interesting and famous books I've worked on as an editor', Robert Giroux, who oversaw the US edition, recalled). Orwell professed himself pleased, but, characteristically, was more concerned by the possibility of practical mishaps. He didn't want to make any changes to the text, he told Moore towards the end of January, but he was anxious that if the Americans went ahead before Warburg he should be sent the proofs to correct himself. A week later he was still fretting about what would in ordinary circumstances have been a routine task. 'I don't suppose it will arise', he told Richard Rees, 'but *if* I should feel very poorly & unequal to correcting proofs, do you think you could do them for me? As there are a lot of neologisms there are bound to be many printers' errors of a stupid kind, & American compositors are very tiresome to deal with as they always think they know better than the author'.

What did the author think of his book? Orwell's capacity for self-criticism can sometimes seem faintly absurd. The uniform edition of his works on which Secker & Warburg had recently embarked would, for example, omit both *A Clergyman's Daughter* (which Orwell described as 'bollix') and *Keep the Aspidistra Flying*, which, he explained to a friend, had simply been written to earn its £100 advance. Here in the early part of 1949 he wrote several teasing letters that disparaged *Nineteen Eighty-Four*'s merits. 'I mucked it up really, partly because I was ill almost throughout the time of writing', he remarked to Dwight Macdonald, the editor of the American magazine *Politics*, 'but some of the ideas in it might interest you perhaps'. To Celia Kirwan he was even more downbeat. 'I will send you a copy of my new book when it comes out . . . but I don't expect you'll like it; it's an awful book really'.

All his worst suspicions of American compositors were realised a fortnight later when the US proofs arrived: chock full of variant spellings and punctuation and with all the metric measurements altered to inches and yards. 'I've already cabled in strong terms', he told Roger Senhouse, his UK editor, 'but I don't like having to fight these battles 3,000 miles from my base'.

On 8 March, Warburg wrote to update him on progress. The book would be published on 14 June, he volunteered (in the event, it appeared on the 8th). The *London Evening Standard* had chosen it as their book for June, as had the selection committee of the Book Society. The post-war British publishing industry was still bedevilled by paper shortages, but Secker had managed to procure enough for a first printing of 25,000 copies and—should sales go as they anticipated—a potential 10,000 copy reprint. The news was followed by a serious downturn in Orwell's health. A few days before, he had brought a letter to Celia Kirwan to a premature end with the words 'I feel so lousy I can't write any more'. By the end of March he was spitting blood—the technical term was *haemoptysis* he told Warburg—and been forbidden to use his typewriter. He recovered slightly, but confessed to Rees that he was 'feeling ghastly most of the time'. Even now, his view of his likely prospects seems to have varied almost from day to day. A letter of 14 April to Robert Giroux paints an optimistic picture of 'being out of here before the summer is over' and having 'my next novel mapped out'. But only 24 hours later, Tosco Fyvel was told that he had been 'horribly ill' and that 'I can't make plans till my health takes a definite turn one way or the other'.

All through the early spring, medical bulletins alternated with excited news from publishers. The US Book of the Month Club, though keen to make *Nineteen Eighty-Four* its summer choice, had wanted changes, notably the removal of the long extract from Emmanuel Goldstein's *The Theory and Practice of Oligarchical Collectivism*. Orwell, who had stood firm, now found his obstinacy rewarded. 'I don't know whether I shall end up with a net profit', he told Rees, 'but at any rate this should pay off my arrears of income tax'. This was a serious underestimate. A Book of the Month Club selection was virtually guaranteed to make its author in excess of £40,000. If he lived, Orwell was set to become a wealthy man. But would he survive? Several of the letters he wrote in mid-April suggest that he was putting plans in place in the event of his death. The letter to Rees about the Book of the Month Club deal goes on to suggest that if things go badly ('of course we hope they won't, but one must be prepared for the worst') he could bring Richard to see him 'before I get too frightening in appearance'. And a long letter to Gwen O'Shaughnessy, sent a week later, canvasses the question of Richard's upbringing: Orwell would be grateful if she and Avril would decide what the best course of action should be if the child were to be orphaned. 'I trust that all this won't become urgent yet awhile', he assured her.

The first copy of *Nineteen Eighty-Four* arrived on 22 April, somewhat to the author's surprise. 'It seems very early for advance copies', he told Warburg. But he liked the jacket, designed by a young protégé of Warburg's named Michael Kennard, and the 'general make-up' and suggested half a dozen literary eminences to whom advance copies might be sent: these included T.S. Eliot, Arthur Koestler, and André Malraux. The letter to Warburg maintains that its writer is 'somewhat better', to the point of being allowed to sit outside in a deckchair when the weather is fine, but ten days later, writing to an American editor who had asked for a piece of journalism, he declared himself 'most deadly ill & quite unable to work'. A letter to David Astor a week after this is grim even by Orwell's standards ('I've been rather bad . . . I've really been very bad'): it wouldn't surprise him if an *Observer* profile Astor was bent on commissioning turned into an obituary. As for the long-term prognosis, 'It looks as if I may have to spend the rest of my life, if not actually in bed, at any rate at the bath-chair level', he told Anthony Powell. He could stand that, he continued, if only he could work. 'At present I can do nothing, not even a book review'.

Warburg, with the finished copies in front of him and the book trade in ferment, alternated encouraging news with concern about his star author's condition. 'I had better report progress', he wrote on 13 May, 'but first I do hope your health is not too shocking'. Unless Secker were living in a world of illusion, he went on, the book was going to be 'a smash hit'. Advance sales had already reached 11,000 copies—this was at a time when the average literary novel routinely sold two or three thousand—while 'all sorts of little indications tend to show that this is the book people are waiting for'. Such was Warburg's confidence that he was preparing to move the publication date forward a week to 8 June as a way of stealing a march on the second volume of Winston Churchill's Second World War trilogy, *Their Finest Hour*, which was due on 27 June ('His book will of course have an enormous sale . . . and we think it is a matter of some importance to get your book well and truly launched as far ahead of his as possible').

Back in Gloucestershire, Orwell had reached an important decision. On their visit four months previously, the Warburgs had pleaded with him to consult Dr Andrew Morland, the specialist who had treated him back in the 1930s, and volunteered to make the arrangements. At the time, on his usual grounds of not wanting to make a fuss, Orwell had turned them down. On 16 May, he finally decided to take them up on their offer. He had been in ghastly health, he explained, too weak even to walk to the X-ray room and stand up against the screen. He had asked Dr Kirkman, the physician immediately responsible for his treatment, if she thought he would survive and she would say only that she didn't know. In these circumstances, once an X-ray of his chest was finally available, he wanted a second opinion. 'They can't do anything, as I'm not a case for an operation'. There was a week's delay, in which letters flew back and forth from Warburg to Cranham and from Cranham to Morland's Harley Street consulting rooms, but on 24 May, Morland travelled down to Gloucestershire to conduct an examination.

The results were less calamitous than Warburg feared. A severe disease in the left lung and a relatively slight amount on the right, Morland reported. If the patient rested properly he ought to improve: on the other hand, it might be that after a number of months he would 'stagnate or relapse'. On one point, Morland was adamant: 'if he ceases to try and get well and settles down to write another book he is almost certain to relapse quickly'. There was no prospect of a complete cure, but ideally Orwell might reach the stage of being regarded as a 'good chronic', able to potter about and do a few hours' work a day in conditions of complete retirement. The state in which he found himself was, Morland insisted, entirely a result of his desperate struggle to finish *Nineteen Eighty-Four* in the winter of 1948: 'His resistance must be fairly good as he stabilized well last year and should not have broken down had he not foolishly over-exercised'. The patient, who wrote to Warburg on the same day, found Morland 'very nice and quite encouraging', but was already fretting at the prospect of a long period of recuperation. What really disturbed him, he confessed to his publisher, was that 'I shall have nothing ready for next year'. Even with the Book of the Month Club's largesse looming over the horizon, his tax arrears paid, and his financial future secure, Orwell the professional writer was still terrified of interrupting his creative flow.

By this point, *Nineteen Eighty-Four* was only a few days away from publication. Rumours of its terrifying subject matter were already circulating around the book trade. Muggeridge noted in his diary that, according to Warburg, several booksellers given advance copies had been so frightened that they had been unable to sleep. Muggeridge, who had read an early copy, found the novel 'rather repugnant' and bearing little relation to life or 'anything that could happen', but this, he soon discovered, was a misjudgement. Most of the novel's early readers were struck by its plausibility, its intimate connection to a world they recognised, its ability to project elements of the life that went on around them into a futuristic nightmare. Their number included Warburg, who had the grace to admit that the original idea he had conceived of the novel was hopelessly misguided. Orwell's initial description of it, back in early 1947—'a fantasy but in the form of a naturalistic novel'—had, he recalled, left him feeling slightly depressed: 'novels about Utopias or anti-Utopias were not my favourite reading, nor the public's'. What he and the tribe of early readers now busy writing their reviews found on their desks was not a book like Huxley's *Brave New World* but a horribly realistic novel about London under a totalitarian dictatorship.

A week before it appeared in the shops, Warburg wrote a reassuring letter, in which the anxieties of a publisher keen that one of his major talents keeps on writing books mingle with the straightforward solicitude of a friend. Provided Orwell kept to the instructions not to overexert himself, Morland's report was encouraging. On the other hand, as Warburg reminded him, 'very definite hopes are held out to you that at a certain stage, not too far away, you can be allowed safely to work on writing several hours a day'. No one could cheat TB: on no account should he start working again until he was given the all-clear. There were so many people who wanted him to stay alive, Warburg continued— Richard, naturally, but also 'your readers, whose numbers will shortly run I hope to hundreds of thousands'. The reviews were pending; soon Secker & Warburg would have 'some slight idea as to sales possibilities'; but the omens looked good. Knowing Orwell's time-honoured habit of fretting about money, Warburg ended up with a flourish. He was convinced, he went on, 'that you will earn in England, and I have no doubt in America too, far more money than from *Animal Farm*, certainly after tax deductions to last you for say three years or more, even allowing for the heavy expenses of treatment in a sanatorium'. There would be more books—a volume of reprinted essays, say, in the autumn of 1950, by which time Orwell might well have recovered sufficiently to begin writing another novel. So the future—or one part of it—was assured. *Nineteen Eighty-Four* would be a huge success. No book published that year could be more relevant to the shape of the post-war world. Financial security was assured. All Orwell had to do was to stay alive.

THERE COMES A MOMENT in the trajectory of an internationally successful book when it tugs free of its moorings, ceases to be narrowly associated with the man or woman who wrote it, sails off into the stratosphere, and takes on a life of its own. With some books this process can take years or even decades to set in train. With *Nineteen Eighty-Four* it seems to have happened almost instantaneously. As Warburg had predicted, the novel was an immediate success—acclaimed by the vast majority of its reviewers and eagerly pursued by the reading public, who flocked in their thousands to buy it. Its power, most English critics agreed, lay in its distance from the H.G. Wells–Aldous Huxley tradition of dystopian fantasy. Rather than fashioning a far-flung never-never land, Orwell had merely projected some of the tendencies he saw around him. 'It is no doubt with the intention of preventing his prediction from coming true', the historian Veronica Wedgwood wrote in *Time and Tide*, 'that Mr Orwell has set it down in the most valuable, the most powerful book he has yet written'.

The *New Statesman*'s V.S. Pritchett commended it a 'satirical pamphlet', as significant as anything Swift had written, and an unrelenting satire on the 'moral corruption of absolute power'. There were occasional complaints about the torture scenes ('melodramatic', 'school-boyish'), but most critics would have agreed with Julian Symons's conclusion that this was a work of universal significance, produced by 'a writer who deals with the problems of the world rather than the ingrowing pains of individuals'. Its prophetic note was warmly commended. To Russell it depicted 'with very great power the horrors of a well-established totalitarian regime of whatever type. It is important that the western world should be aware of these dangers'. Rebecca West, voting *Nineteen Eighty-Four* her book of the year, thought that it 'succeeded in depicting not only a set of circumstances, but how characters would react to them'. So, too, was its contention that the growth of totalitarian regimes took root in the collapse of religious belief. Most important of all its achievements, the *Catholic Herald* declared, was its 'analysis of the underlying motive which keeps the wheels going in this triumphant totalitarian world . . . the lust of power'. In getting to the heart of the totalitarian mind, Orwell had come 'full circle on history to the fall of the Angels and the fall of man'.

As fan letters rolled in from literary peers, sales followed suit. Secker had printed a first edition of 25,575 copies, followed this up with a second impression of 5,570 copies, and then ordered a further 5,150. In America, Harcourt, Brace and Company began with an initial print run of 20,000 copies, and two follow-up impressions of 10,000 each. The US Book of the Month Club edition, which appeared in July, sold 190,000 copies in a little over eighteen months. By the early autumn there were Spanish, Swedish, Japanese, French, and Danish versions in the offing. A German translation was published in the recently established intellectual monthly *Der Monat*. Meanwhile, American enthusiasm for the novel produced, in quick succession, an NBC broadcast, a *Reader's Digest* condensed version, and proposals for a Broadway play. Orwell had no objection, 'although I should not have thought it lent itself to stage treatment'. On the other hand, he presciently remarked, 'I should think it ought to be filmable'.

Part of *Nineteen Eighty-Four*'s success lay in the political backdrop against which it appeared: the sharply contested ideological landscape of the 1940s in which the form of tyranny represented by German Fascism seemed to have been replaced by an alternative version pioneered by Soviet Communism. Conservatives liked it for confirming their worst suspicions about Stalin. At a time when the British Labour Party harboured at least a dozen 'fellow-travelling' MPs who took their orders from

Communist Party headquarters in King Street, democratic left-wingers admired it for drawing attention to some of the dangers of an autocratic government in command of a centralised economy, and for exposing the totalitarian assault on the concept of objective truth. Detractors tended to be out-and-out Communists, such as the critic in *Reynold's News*, a left-leaning UK Sunday paper, who maintained that its aim was simply to stir up enmity against the Soviet Union and located the author on the 'lunatic fringe' of the Labour Party.

All this, though, is to ignore the novel's well-nigh visceral impact on its original audience. It was not just that, four years into the Cold War with Soviet puppet regimes installed in every legislature in Eastern Europe, *Nineteen Eighty-Four* touched an ideological nerve. At the same time, it struck hard at the imagination of thousands of individual readers. A doomed love affair; a devastating analysis of the corruption of language; an exploration of the depths of human psychology; a dystopian horror world: Orwell's novel is all these things and more—a glittering futurist extravaganza of tall buildings and circling helicopters which is, simultaneously, populated by characters who would have seemed perfectly at home in the bomb-cratered London streets of 1948. Many of the book's first readers left accounts of the way in which *Nineteen Eighty-Four* affected them. They range from David Pryce-Jones, the 13-year-old son of the *Times Literary Supplement*'s editor, who having browsed delightedly through his father's proof, immediately petitioned his school librarian for a copy, to John Dos Passos, who wrote to tell the author that he had 'read it with such cold shivers as I haven't had since as a child I read Swift about the Yahoos. Had nightmares all next week about two way television'.

What did Orwell make of *Nineteen Eighty-Four*'s success? He was certainly pleased by its reception, while lamenting what he called 'some very shame-making publicity'. He was also desperate to get back to work. Warburg, visiting him at Cranham in mid-June, produced another long internal memorandum for his colleagues which ends with the paragraph 'Ability to Write'. The effort of turning ideas in his head into rough drafts was work which he could not afford to attempt for several months, Warburg reported. 'At worst he has a 50/50 chance of recovering and living for a number of years', he concluded. 'Probably everything depends on himself and he does at last realise what is involved and what he has got to do'. Under 'Literary Work', he noted a scheme for 'a nouvelle [sic] of 30,000 to 40,000 words—a novel of character rather than of ideas, with Burma as background. George was naturally as reticent as usual, but he did disclose this much'.

But George was fading away. All that survives of the novella, which was to have been called 'A Smoking-room Story', are a page or two of notes in which a young man named Curly Johnson returns to England on the boat from Burma in the late 1920s, just as Orwell himself had done two decades before. Assessing his chances at the end of May, Morland had warned of the danger that he might 'stagnate' or relapse. Over the next six months his condition underwent a slow deterioration which no amount of medical care could alleviate. 'I have Morland coming to see me again this evening', he wrote to Warburg on 22 August. 'On and off I've been feeling absolutely ghastly. It comes and goes, but I have periodic bouts of high temperatures'. Two weeks later he was brought back to London by private ambulance and installed at Morland's private fiefdom of University College London. The same letter talks of Orwell's intention of 'getting married again (to Sonia) when I am once again in the land of the living, if ever I am. I suppose everyone will be horrified, but apart from other considerations I really think I should stay alive longer if I were married'.

Once the news had got out, most of Orwell's friends were puzzled rather than horrified by his second marriage. Few of them knew Sonia. Those who did remembered the rather bossy, efficient young woman who ran the *Horizon* office in Connolly's absence and wondered at the bridegroom's enthusiasm ('Whole affair is slightly macabre and incomprehensible', Muggeridge wrote in his diary). The majority of them were won round by her obvious devotion to Orwell and her punctiliousness in managing his affairs. As there could be no question of Orwell attending a church, the ceremony took place in his hospital room. David Astor officiated as 'best man'. A champagne bottle sat incongruously beside the medical equipment. A friend of Sonia's recalled an atmosphere of 'bleakness and touching sadness. I think I had tears in my eyes watching that ill, smiling face'. Though cheered by his marriage, he grew steadily weaker. It became difficult to give him penicillin injections as so little spare flesh remained in which to jab the needle. He had got so thin, he told Celia Kirwan, 'that it's below the level at which you can go on living'. Muggeridge, visiting him with Powell on Christmas Day, thought that he resembled a picture he had once seen of Nietzsche on his deathbed. There was a scheme to transport Orwell to a sanatorium in the Swiss alps—not, it was quietly assumed, that the alpine air would have any effect on his lungs. The aim was to smooth the circumstances of his passing: the fishing rods that might have accompanied him lay in the corner of his hospital room on the night he died.

Orwell's will had stipulated that his funeral service should follow the rites of the Church of England and that he should be buried in a cemetery. Given that he had no known Christian beliefs or affiliations, both these requests were difficult to accomplish. In the end Anthony Powell and his wife enlisted the vicar of Christ Church, Albany Street, to conduct the service, while David Astor procured a burial plot in the graveyard of the Oxfordshire village of Sutton Courtenay that adjoined the Astor family's estate. Both these ceremonies were conducted on 26 January 1950. By now the obituaries had begun to pour in: 'the wintry conscience of a generation', Pritchett declared in the *New Statesman*. The process of winding up his estate creaked slowly into gear. The farmhouse at Barnhill was given up. Richard, age five and a half, was consigned to the care of his aunt Avril. Sonia began on a flamboyant and latterly somewhat melancholy 30-year career as 'the Widow Orwell'. The book continued on its meteoric flight.

PART III

After (1949 ad infinitum)

7. COLD WAR WARRIORS

ORWELL HAD KNOWN that there would trouble over *Nineteen Eighty-Four*. As it turned out, the first transatlantic salvos descended on his pillow-bound head at Cranham only a few days after the book was published. As early as 22 June 1949 he could be found warning his anarchist friend Vernon Richards that he was afraid 'some of the U.S. Republican papers have tried to use "1984" as propaganda against the Labour Party, but I have issued a sort of démenti which I hope will be printed'. If authorial alarm bells had been set off by an article in the *New York Daily News*, then Orwell and his publisher were equally displeased by some of the political implications of an illustrated summary of the novel which had appeared in *Life* beneath the heading 'An Englishman writes a frightening satire about the cruel fate of man in a regimented left-wing police state which controls his mind and soul'. This might well have been interpreted as an assault on the Labour government of Clement Attlee, whose four years in office had been marked by a comprehensive programme of economic centralisation, symbolised by the taking private industries into state control. But students of the US political scene noted that the magazine had widened its range of attack for the benefit of a more domestic audience. *Nineteen Eighty-Four*, as reimagined by *Life*'s pro-Republican proprietor Henry Luce, was, at least by implication, an exposure of the essential totalitarianism of Roosevelt's National Industrial

Recovery Act, a withering critique of 'those fervent New Dealers in the United States [who] often seemed to have the secret hope that the depression mentality of the 1930s, source of their power and excuse for their experiments, would never end'.

'So far as the Right is concerned', the political journalist Peregrine Worsthorne once declared, 'Orwell can do no wrong'. It is possible to detect the origins of the almost legendary status that *Nineteen Eighty-Four* was to acquire among banner wavers of the Anglo-American right here in June 1949. Orwell, though dangerously ill, was desperate to correct the misinformation then circulating in the American right-wing press. To this end, a week or so after the first batch of US reviews had appeared, he instructed Fred Warburg to issue a statement correcting the widespread assumption that the book was a forecast of the probable shape of the western world forty years on. Orwell's view, alternatively, was that 'allowing for the book being after all a parody, something like NINETEEN EIGHTY-FOUR *could* happen'. The danger lay in the structure imposed on both left- and right-wing capitalist societies by 'the necessity to prepare for total war with the U.S.S.R. and the new weapons. Of which of course the atom bomb is the most powerful and the most publicized'. The moral to be drawn from this nightmare situation was a simple one: '*Don't let it happen. It depends on you*'. An even brisker summary of what Orwell assumed his political position to be appears in a second statement, conveyed to the president of the United Automobile Workers Union (UAW), who wanted to recommend the book to its members but needed ideological reassurance.

My novel *Nineteen Eighty-Four* is *not* intended as an attack on socialism, or on the British Labour party, but as a show-up of the perversions to which a centralised economy is liable, and which have already been realised in Communism and fascism. I do not believe that the kind of society I describe necessarily *will* arrive, but I believe (allowing of course for the fact that the book is a satire) that something resembling it *could* arrive. I believe also that totalitarian ideas have taken root in the minds of intellectuals everywhere, and I have tried to draw these ideas out to their logical consequences. The scene of the book is laid in Britain in order to emphasize that the English-speaking races are not innately better than anyone else and that totalitarianism, if not fought against, could triumph anywhere.

The Warburg statement, though telephoned to *Life*, remained unused. Instead, Luce and his henchmen managed to muddy the waters still further by reproducing the message to the UAW and making it look like a direct letter from Orwell to the magazine. Meanwhile, more discerning American readers had already grasped that the book was not exclusively anti-Communist but anti-totalitarian. One of the last correspondences in which Orwell ever engaged, shortly before his transfer from Cranham to University College Hospital in the early autumn of 1949, was with the young American screenwriter (and later bestselling novelist) Sidney Sheldon, who had proposed to adapt the novel for the Broadway stage. In the end the project came to nothing, but Sheldon was determined to give his adaptation an anti-fascist slant: Orwell supported him in this, and was keen enough on Sheldon's original proposals to give him a fair amount of leeway (a letter to Leonard Moore from late August notes that 'it would put him in an intolerable position if I had to approve all last-minute changes suggested for producers etc. I would be satisfied if I could see & approve the first draft, provided that it is agreed that the general tendency of the adaptation is not radically altered'). Like many a novelist whose work is about to be snapped up by another branch of the media, Orwell was nervous that, as he put it, 'the meaning of the book might be seriously deformed', but Shelden's understanding of its ideological targets seems to have reassured him: 'from the letter he wrote me recently I don't think he intends doing this'.

But there was another way in which American conservatives—British conservatives, if it came to that—had failed to understand *Nineteen Eighty-Four*'s central point. Fred Warburg, in summarising the novel for his colleagues, had assumed that its message was entirely pessimistic: 'Orwell has no hope, or at least he allows his reader no tiny flickering candlelight of hope'. Towards the end of the report, this point is reiterated: in the torture scenes at the Ministry of Love, 'Orwell is concerned to obliterate hope; there will be no rebellion, there cannot be any liberation'. To the publisher 'Orwell goes down to the depths in a way which reminds me of Dostoievsky. O'Brien is the Grand Inquisitor, and he leaves Winston, and the reader, without hope'. Looking back on his original summary from the vantage point of 1973, Warburg decided that there was little in it that he wanted to alter, with the possible exception of his belief that Orwell was making 'a deliberate and sadistic attack on socialism and socialist parties generally'. To conservatively minded readers who came across the book in the 1950s, the novel's end-of-tether quality and its apparent air of hopelessness was a key element in its allure. A dystopian projection of a Socialist regime had to end in misery, constraint, or oppression, or where was the value of the capitalist system it had replaced?

But *Nineteen Eighty-Four* is not entirely without its occasional glances at the prospect of a better world. To begin with, there is its teasing twelve-page appendix on 'The Principles of Newspeak'. Written exclusively in the past tense, at some indeterminate future point—it refers, for example, to the 'final, perfected version' embodied in the Eleventh Edition of the official Newspeak Dictionary on which Winston's colleague Syme is working at the time of his liquidation—this appears to be work of some linguistic historian coolly appraising a bygone phenomenon. The conclusions of the piece are tantalising in their ambiguity, and the reader is perfectly entitled to assume that when the anonymous author writes that 'it was expected that Newspeak would have finally superseded Oldspeak (or Standard English, as we should call it) by about the year 2050', the author is implying that this moment never occurred, that Newspeak has been, gone, and is now regarded as an historical curiosity.

This is not Orwell's only hint that the Oceania of the future may be a very different place. The thrilling moment at which O'Brien assures Winston that 'we shall meet in the place where there's no darkness' may well be the prelude to a nightmare descent into betrayal and humiliation—a horribly ironic prelude, too, as the place where O'Brien and Winston re-encounter each other is the brightly lit torture chamber of the Ministry of Love. But it is still a thrilling moment, for it conveys the faint suggestion that at some point the shadows that hang over Oceania will be dispersed. In much the same way, the scene in which Winston observes the prole woman hanging out the washing in her ramshackle backyard and embarks on his long reverie about a future time at which their strength 'will change into consciousness' is clearly a crucial part of Orwell's feelings about the novel. 'The proles were immortal', Winston reflects, 'you could not doubt it when you looked at that valiant figure in the yard. In the end their awakening would come'. Even more important, perhaps, is Winston's first glimpse of the woman, a chapter or two before, where he begins to discern the proles' political importance. Untouched by the tides of history, the rise of Oceania and the formal life of Airstrip One, governed by private rather than communal loyalties, they are still, at least potentially, agents for change. Or rather more than this, for they have retained a vital, elemental quality which Winston and his fellow members of the Inner Party have lost.

> The proles, it suddenly occurred to him, had remained in this condition. They were not loyal to a party or a country or an idea, they were loyal to one another. For the first time in his life he did not despise the proles or think of them merely as an inert force which would one day spring to life and regenerate the world. The proles had stayed human. They had not become hardened inside. They had held on to the primitive emotions which he himself had to re-learn by conscious effort.

'The proles are human beings', he tells Julia. 'We are not human'. The process by which the proles become radicalised and fulfil their destiny may take centuries, but the result will be worth waiting for, 'because at the least it would be a world of sanity. Where there is equality there can be sanity'. Here in the dystopian world of Oceania, Orwell is essentially restating the message of *The Lion and the Unicorn: Socialism and the English Genius*, the pamphlet written in the early years of the war. A centralised economy of the kind required for a nation state to prosper in the modern age can only survive by meeting the needs of all its citizens, and it can only do this by treating them all on equal terms. However demoralising its central premise and however disquieting the terrors released on its central character, down on *Nineteen Eighty-Four*'s unregarded edge, there are still stray glimmers of light pulsing on through the darkness.

There is at least a possibility that some of these glimmers may pulse through Winston Smith. In the original UK Secker & Warburg edition, as Winston sits listlessly playing chess in the novel's final chapter, he traces in the dust of the table-top '2 + 2 ='. As the marked-up typescripts, the corrected proofs, and all the US editions contain the equation in its completed form ('2 + 2 = 5'), this is usually assumed to have been a printer's error. As Peter Davison remarks in his authoritative edition of the text, 'Lack of the "5" negates Orwell's point that Winston has submitted without reservation to Big Brother'.

ONE OF THE MOST significant aspects of *Nineteen Eighty-Four*'s long afterlife is the sheer pace of its collective take-up. By as early as the mid-1950s it not only had acquired a vast international audience—sales of the American paperback edition between 1950 and 1957 amounted to well over a million copies—but also had metamorphosed into a moral yardstick: one of those rare books by which a political regime, a technological innovation, and sometimes even a solitary human act can be judged and found wanting. Naturally, the novel's first post-war readership found a variety of different things to admire, or to be frightened by, in it. To a Cold War intellectual, it was a dazzling projection of some of the oligarchical and hegemonic tendencies of an economically centralised state. To a library subscriber in a provincial English town it was a dystopia of the kind that Wells had popularised half a century before given a frightening realistic sheen. To a politician, it was an all-too-believable prefiguration of the post-war world. Calling at 10 Downing Street in February 1953, Churchill's doctor Lord Moran 'found the P.M. absorbed in George Orwell's book 1984'. Had he read it? Churchill straightaway inquired. 'I'm reading it for a second time. It's a very remarkable book'. To the 7.1-million-strong audience (this included the Queen and Prince Philip) who watched the first UK TV adaptation in December 1954, it was simply two hours of high-grade entertainment courtesy of a medium that had yet to achieve very much in the way of public impact.

Another mark of the novel's resonance was the speed with which its key inventions began to take up residence in the public imagination. In his essay on Dickens, Orwell himself makes the point that 'until fairly recently'—he was writing in 1939—a comedian who went on stage in a northern variety hall and began to imitate one of Dickens's better-known characters could be sure of being understood: such was the allure of Fagin, Miss Havisham, and Bill Sikes that they were recognisable even to people who had never come across them in print. By the mid-1950s, much the same could be said of Orwell's imagined world. As Anthony Burgess once put it: 'There are many who, not knowing Orwell's novel *Nineteen Eighty-Four*, nevertheless know such terms as doublethink and Newspeak and Big Brother, and, above all, associate the cipher 1984 with a situation in which the individual has lost all his rights of moral choice . . . and is subject to the arbitrary power of some ruling body—not necessarily the State'. This tendency became yet more marked in the early 2000s, in the wake of mass-audience TV shows in which symbols of totalitarian oppression were reinvented to suit the demands of popular entertainment. In *Big Brother*, for example, television cameras track the every movement of the inhabitants of the 'Big Brother House'; *Room 101* features celebrities complaining about their particular pet hates. But even in the Eisenhower era the average newspaper reader would have known what was meant by the adjective 'Orwellian'—something intrusive, malign, repressive, hierarchical, anxious to snuff out individual liberty, abetting a spurious communality against solitary self-determination.

To add to this, as the post-war era ground on, was the question of Orwell's prescience, the idea that he had sketched out in fiction a whole host of phenomena that now seemed to be rooted in fact. *Nineteen Eighty-Four* may have been intended as a 'warning' rather than a prophecy, but no observer of the third and fourth quarters of the twentieth century—their social tendencies as much as their geopolitics—could fail to be struck by the accuracy of its forecasts. The distinguished Orwell scholar Peter Davison once compiled a by no means exhaustive list of the things that 'Orwell got right'. They included: the division of the world into endlessly contending mini-empires and zones of influence, often squaring up to each other in proxy wars fought by satellites; the steady rise of an unregulated surveillance culture designed to limit the individual's liberty of movement and a person's right to self-expression, and the psychological consequences of this intrusion; the increasing prevalence of leadership cults; environmental degradation; deforestation; the demoralisation of large parts of society through the circulation of pornography; lack of privacy; alienation; the consistent tampering with matters of recorded fact for ideological purposes; and a great deal more besides.

Inevitably, much of *Nineteen Eighty-Four*'s landscape is generalised rather than particular; it is perfectly possible, with an atlas of early-twenty-first-century international history before one, to demonstrate quite how little exact resemblance the world of Oceania, Eurasia, and Eastasia bears to our own. In his long preface to *1985* (1978), a dystopian novel deliberately conceived in Orwell's shadow, Anthony Burgess combs through the novel on a point-by-point basis to establish that nearly every warning Orwell has pronounced needs to be qualified into virtual non-existence ('Let's be sensible. There's nothing in the traditions of the United States which predisposes them to authoritarianism on the European model . . . there's a lot of power about but it's not centralised on the Ingsoc pattern', etc.). But there is a way in which recent history can make this kind of deflation seem oddly superfluous. At any rate, the twenty-first-century British citizen who takes the train into work in the morning, to arrive at a town whose principal economic outlet is a nearby USAF base, walks through streets festooned with CCTV cameras, and buys a newspaper on whose front page is a story about illicit data-harvesting by a big technology company, a report of some of President Trump's complaints about 'fake news', and a statement by him (in the wake of a hurricane that has laid waste to the Southern states) to the effect that the contemporary climate is 'glorious' might be forgiven for thinking that Orwell knew what he was talking about.

For the moment, in the 1950s, only a few years into the novel's protracted lifespan, much of this awareness lay in the future.

The real boost to *Nineteen Eighty-Four*'s prodigious success in the two decades after the war lay in its deployment, by US government agencies, as a weapon in the Cold War. Whatever might be inferred about totalitarianism in general from the descriptions of life in Oceania, a CIA propagandist who leafed through them in search of ammunition would have been instantly aware of quite how specific was their relationship to the Stalinist regime of the late 1940s. The 'Junior Spies', for example, are based on the widely reported phenomenon of patriotic Russian children denouncing their parents to the authorities. 'Facecrime', a misdemeanour arising from a gesture or a facial expression, echoes an instruction issued in Moscow in 1949 to the effect that 'one must not content oneself with merely paying attention to what is being said . . . One must pay attention to the manner—to the sincerity, for example, with which a schoolmistress recites a poem the authorities regard as doubtful'. 'Doublethink', as Robert Conquest observes, is an almost literal translation of the Russian *dvoeverye*, or 'dual faith', a phrase originally used to describe the survival of pagan practices alongside, and sometimes within, Christian belief.

Valuable as this information was to the American government, it needed careful handling. As several historians of immediately post-war international relations have pointed out, US public opinion in the late 1940s was not at all anti-Soviet. To millions of Americans, Russia was a gallant ally ('Stalin wasn't stallin' / when he told the beast of Berlin / that they'd never rest contented / till they'd driven him from the land' ran a comradely close-harmony hit song from 1943 by the Golden Gate Jubilee Quartet), whose ideological flaws could be forgiven for their contribution to the war effort. This, though, was the era of the Truman Doctrine and the Marshall Plan, with their political and economic support for non-Communist governments of Europe threatened by Soviet infiltration. An essential part of Truman's, and later Eisenhower's, strategy was to drum up anti-Soviet feeling. Significantly, these efforts took place not only in the political sphere, but also in the world of popular culture as well.

Certainly, no one who watched the fifty-minute CBS dramatization of *Nineteen Eighty-Four* screened live in 1953, shortly after Stalin's death, could have doubted its political undertones. There was no hint that Airstrip One was in London. American accents abounded. Goldstein was clearly intended to be Trotsky, and Big Brother, in the words of the film historian David Ryan, resembled 'something *Mad* magazine commissioned from Picasso'. Nonetheless, the play was a ratings hit, watched in nearly 9 million American homes and achieving an outstanding 53 per cent of market share. To emphasize its propaganda value, *Life* ran a picture spread featuring rehearsal photos. In a further anti-Communist twist, the director, Paul Nickell, later remarked that his aim had been to instil a subconscious link between the novel and Senator Joseph McCarthy's ongoing 'Red Scare'. Ominously, the girl who played Parsons's eavesdropping daughter, who denounces him to the authorities after hearing him murmur the words 'Down with Big Brother' in his sleep, said that when she watched the McCarthy hearings a year later she was reminded of *Nineteen Eighty-Four*.

If no state agency was actively involved in the CBS adaptation, then the persistent early-1950s effort to transform the novel into a feature film—or rather a feature film that would promote a government-endorsed view of Russia—can be traced directly to the CIA's Office of Policy Coordination. Two members of its Psychological Warfare Workshop (PWW) had already travelled to England to meet Sonia and persuade her to sign over the rights to *Animal Farm*. Famously, Orwell's fable of a revolution that fails metamorphosed into an animated film with a different ending, in which the non-pig population of the farm whip up a rebel army, storm the farmhouse, and send their oppressors packing. To the PWW, *Nineteen Eighty-Four* looked an even more attractive proposition. Happily for them, the film rights were by now in the hands of a McCarthyite sympathiser named Peter Rathvon of the Motion Picture Capital Corporation. Liaising with another instrument of government propaganda, the recently formed United States Information Agency, the PWW brokered a deal whereby Rathvon would be offered a $100,000 subsidy and guaranteed world rights provided that its executives could superintend the writing of the screenplay.

Something of the air of propagandist micromanagement brought to the proceedings can be glimpsed in the relationship between Rathvon and yet another right-wing pressure group active in the 1950s culture wars, the American Committee for Cultural Freedom (ACCF), whose executive director Sol Stein was consulted about the script. Stein was adamant that the storyline should not be established in some futurist other-world, but should 'have a great deal of relevance to the specifics of present day totalitarianism'—that is, the variety on display beyond the Iron Curtain. To this end, he counselled, the posters of Big Brother should display photographs of an actual human being, rather than a cartoon caricature of the recently deceased Stalin. To Stein, the object should be a meticulously observed verisimilitude, shunning exaggeration or dramatic heightening for 'an extension of something we can directly witness today'. There was, for example, a difficulty about the sashes worn by the members of the Junior Anti-Sex League. As nothing comparable could be found in Eastern Europe, he advised that Julia should instead be kitted out with an armband.

Much more problematic was the novel's finale, in which a broken-down and demoralised Winston admits that he has won the battle over himself, and that he loves Big Brother. On the one hand, the paladins of the ACCF were keen that the supposed realities of life in the Soviet Union be brought home to domestic audiences as remorselessly as possible. On the other, they were aware that the vast majority of American cinemagoers were less interested in ideological purity than an upbeat ending. Stein's solution was for Winston (played by Edmond O'Brien), leaving the café in which he and Julia (Jan Sterling) have met for the last time, to head off in the opposite direction to her. On the way, he encounters a group of children who, against the odds, Stein suggests, 'have managed to maintain some of their natural innocence'. Eventually, he finds the rural refuge in which he and Julia first contrived to evade Big Brother's all-seeing eye. The camera lingers over blades of grass. Wind is heard sighing in the trees, together with the beat of Winston's heart. These, we infer, are the things that rampant autocracy cannot take away from its citizenry, 'and perhaps to clinch this point of view, we can see Winston looking at his hands: two fingers on his left hand, two fingers on his right, and he knows that two plus two make four'.

Sadly, there was to be no lingering over blades of grass, and no windblown treetops. Rathvon vetoed the idea. To appease his CIA paymasters, he filmed two alternative endings. Each begins with the ex-lovers meeting in Victory Square. In the first, Winston joins a mob chanting the words 'Long Live Big Brother'. In the second, he defiantly yells 'Down with Big Brother', is shot by vengeful soldiery, but is reunited with Julia who, running to join him and bending over his prostrate form, reaches for his hand amid swirling autumn leaves. To solve the dilemma of which audiences should be allowed to view which interpretations, the film's distributors were given a free vote: American audiences saw the obedient chanting; British viewers made do with outstretched hands and autumn leaves.

Producers, backers, and distributors had high hopes for the finished product. In this Anglo-American production, filmed in London and the Home Counties, with Victory Square carefully reassembled on the Elstree Studios set, Sol Stein reposed the greatest confidence. Both *Animal Farm* and *Nineteen Eighty-Four*, he pronounced, were 'of ideological interest to the American Committee for Cultural Freedom'. Promising to ensure that each got as 'wide distribution as possible', he embarked on a range of promotional sorties, including 'arranging for editorials in New York newspapers' and distribution of 'a very large quantity of discount coupons'. All these efforts were of little avail. Marketed as a science-fiction thriller in the US, where it was released on a double bill with the B-movie *The Gamma People*, *Nineteen Eighty-Four* was poorly received by the critics and flopped at the box office.

However ultimately unsuccessful, Rathvon's adaptation served one useful purpose. This was to highlight the backdrop against which both small- and wide-screen versions of the novel would find themselves having to operate. It had also exposed some of the procedural dilemmas to which many of them would be subject. How, when it came to it, should Orwell's text be approached on film? As a piece of futuristic prophecy, welded to some of the conventions of contemporary sci-fi? As a realistic satire? A mixture of the two? Should one actively embrace the propagandist elements that zealots were keen to attach to it or attempt to let the story speak for itself? How much of the story—in particular Winston's torture at the Ministry of Love— was actually filmable? And how did one deal with the controversy that seemed, almost inevitably, to follow in its wake? Significantly, many of these questions had already been given an airing in the attempt on *Nineteen Eighty-Four* by the BBC, whose two near-identical versions were broadcast live in December 1954.

Filmed on a budget of £3,000, and starring several British actors who would go on to forge substantial careers in film and television (Peter Cushing as Winston, Donald Pleasance as O'Brien, Wilfrid Brambell of *Steptoe and Son* in a cameo as the old man Winston meets in the pub), the BBC production looks as if its director, Rudolph Cartier, had originally intended to play up the science-fiction angle: its writer, Nigel Kneale, was a veteran of the immensely successful six-part *The Quatermass Experiment*, in which a rocket scientist accidently releases a giant space monster; the interiors of the Ministry of Love could easily be mistaken for space laboratories. Each screening was preceded by an announcement: 'More than anything else, this story is a warning, an imaginative picture of the sort of world that might come into being when man loses all that he believes to be right and just'. As for the controversy, there were complaints about Winston's torture, by means of a rat cage connected to a transparent helmet by way of rubber tubing, and a female viewer in Kent was alleged to have died of a heart attack brought on by sheer fright. Meanwhile the propagandist element was reinforced by a parliamentary motion put forward by half a dozen Conservative MPs which congratulated the Corporation for attempting 'to bring home to the British people the logical and soul-destroying consequences of surrendering their freedom and [calling] attention to the fact that many of the inhuman practices depicted in the play *Nineteen Eighty-Four* are already in use under totalitarian regimes'.

Left-wing newspapers, suspecting a capitalist plot, were quick to retaliate. The Communist *Daily Worker* denounced the novel as 'a Tory guttersnipe's view of socialism' and accused once-critical journalists of changing sides once they divined that *Animal Farm* and *Nineteen Eighty-Four* were 'the Old and New Testaments of intellectuals who'd sold out to capitalism'. Nonetheless, all the evidence suggests that, as in the US, it was the BBC broadcast that brought a novel previously available only as an expensive hardback to a mass audience. The two broadcasts of Cartier's play were seen by nearly a fifth of the UK population. Many more people would have read about it in the accompanying press coverage. There was an immediate effect on sales: booksellers disposed of 18,000 copies of the newly published Penguin paperback in the following week. And all this is to ignore the instant, visceral impact on the millions of individual viewers transfixed by the shots of Winston Smith with his gaze turned on the cage of starving rats. My father remembered his mother—like much of the original audience, a recent convert to television—watching it in a state of disbelieving terror.

IF, COME THE MID-1950s, *Nineteen Eighty-Four* had acquired a mass audience, whether as book, film, or TV play, then, higher up the intellectual ladder, it had also begun to colonise several other influential groups of readers. On the one hand, it was a book with which the Right could chastise the Left. But it was also a book with which the Left—or certain remorseful elements of the Left—could chastise itself. One of the key intellectual developments of the 1950s and the two decades that followed it was the habit of one-time left-wingers to jump ship. Sometimes the stimulus was a single, indefensible event—the Soviet suppression of the 1956 Hungarian uprising, say. At other times, the process was infinitely more gradual: the English novelist Kingsley Amis, for example, migrated from war-era membership of the British Communist Party to the mid-1950s authorship of a pro-Labour Fabian Society pamphlet entitled *Socialism and the Intellectuals* and a final vote for Labour at the 1964 general election before switching his support to the Conservatives. While it is easy to overstate the influence of particular writers—and particular books—on shifts of political allegiance, Orwell's effect on the dozens of writers who abandoned their positions on the left can be detected in half a dozen memoirs of the post-war cultural scene.

This process was rarely straightforward. Frequently it involved recalibrating assumptions made several years before. In 1969, for example, having written an article praising *Nineteen Eighty-Four* in the right-leaning *Daily Express*, Amis was contacted by a fan who asked him how he could reconcile his enthusiasm with the Fabian pamphlet, which accuses Orwell of 'warning the late Forties of something already averted in the late Thirties'. Not only does Amis's reply illustrate the slow waning-away of his youthful radicalism; it also demonstrates the part that Orwell had played in inspiring his long march into right-wing exile:

I think that in the late '50s, when I still retained considerable vestiges of my early Leftism, I was made uncomfortable by Orwell's writings about Communism. I could not dismiss him as dishonest or callow, so found an 'out' by calling him hysterical. I think now that (understandably) Orwell had made a better prediction in 1949 than I was capable of in 1959, and my rating of *Nineteen Eighty-Four* as political writing is much higher now than it was then.

What Orwell might have thought of the tribe of ex-leftists who regarded *Nineteen Eighty-Four* as the instrument of their political about-face can only be guessed at (it is worth pointing out, in this context, that conservative friends who survived him hazarded that, had he lived, he would have supported such post-Imperial initiatives as the Falklands War and opposed striking miners). But he would have warmly approved of another small, but ever-growing audience who were introduced to the novel in the early 1950s. This was the *samizdat* (literally 'self-published', in this case clandestinely and illegally) readership of Eastern Europe, where underground editions began to appear almost as soon as early copies had been smuggled out of the West. Poorly produced on cheap paper, often mis-paginated or with all the print shifted to the right-hand page, samizdat Orwell achieved a wide circulation throughout the next three and a half decades, with praise for the novel's message frequently alternating with bewilderment that someone who had never lived under Communism could so comprehensively have imagined some of its terrors. As the Polish poet and essayist Czeslaw Milosz put it:

A few have become acquainted with Orwell's 1984; because it is both difficult to obtain and dangerous to possess, it is known only to certain members of the Inner Party. Orwell fascinates them through his insight into details they know well, and through his use of Swiftian satire . . . Even those who know Orwell only by hearsay are amazed that a writer who never lived in Russia should have so keen a perception into its life.

Milosz is writing as early as 1951–2, in a book published in the West in 1953, but the point continued to be made until the collapse of the Berlin Wall. As Christopher Hitchens has noted, almost all the homegrown champions of Eastern European freedom, from Milosz to Vaclav Havel, Leszek Kolakowski, and Adam Michnik, at one time or another paid tribute to Orwell as a beacon who had lit them on their way. Meanwhile, O'Brien's vision of the post-1984 world—'If you want a picture of the future, imagine a boot stamping on a human face forever'—became an enduring image for the Soviet stifling of dissent behind the Iron Curtain. Researching his memoir of Orwell published in 1982, Tosco Fyvel discovered that the passage turned up in nearly every commemoration of anti-Russian agitation brought to the printed page: in articles on the tenth anniversary of the overthrow of Dubcek's liberal-minded regime in Czechoslovakia; on the twenty-fifth anniversary of the suppression of the Hungarian rising of 1956; on the crushing of the Polish Solidarity movement in 1981–2. Brezhnev, the Soviet leader, was even quoted as remarking that 'the Soviet boot must be on the face of the satellite countries forever'.

All this gave Orwell a unique status in the Eastern Europe of the post-war era. The historian Timothy Garton-Ash remembered that in his travels beyond the pre-glasnost Iron Curtain, 'all over Communist Europe, readers would show me their dog-eared copies of *Animal Farm* and *Nineteen Eighty-Four* and ask "How did he know?"' Everywhere they looked in Soviet daily life of the Cold War era, samizdat readers could see state-sanctioned horrors or inanities that Orwell seemed to have anticipated. What, after all, could have been more Orwellian than the official response to the aftermath of the Chernobyl disaster of April 1986 when, with radiation levels in the surrounding area rising by the hour, *Pravda* printed a statement claiming that the situation was improving, news of the worst nuclear accident in history eventually surfaced in the *New York Times*, and nearly a third of Soviet media coverage was aimed not at reporting the facts of the case but disputing Western exaggerations of their scale?

ALL THIS SERVES to illustrate one of *Nineteen Eighty-Four*'s most abiding characteristics: its protean quality. A faintly exasperated Bernard Crick once itemised the varieties of interpretation to which it could be subjected: 'deterministic prophecy, as a kind of science fiction or a dystopia, as a conditional projection of the future, as a humanistic satire on contemporary events, as a total rejection of socialism of any kind, and as a libertarian socialist—almost an anarchist—protest against totalitarian tendencies and abuses of power both in his own and other possible societies'. Published in 1949, it was at least as, if not more, applicable to the world of the mid-1980s. David Dwan has noted the almost monotonous regularity with which, for example, it has been invoked in the British Houses of Parliament. The Special Powers Act of 1972 ('the embodiment of George Orwell's 1984'), the Data Protection Bill of 1983 ('George Orwell's 1984 come to life'), the Community Charges Bill of 1990 ('an Orwellian dream come true'), the Gender Recognition Act of 2004 ('an Orwellian nightmare'), the Counter-Terrorism and Security Act of 2015 ('how Orwell would have shuddered')—all were put to the Orwell test by parliamentarians and found conspicuously wanting. It was the same with liberal American responses to the post-9/11 use of the Patriot Act to investigate the activities of potential terrorists: the licence given to federal agents to seize computers and pore over suspects' papers amounted to 'Orwellian surveillance', according to Bernie Sanders.

That many of the politicians and social commentators who so regularly pressed *Nineteen Eighty-Four* into service on their behalf had not gone so far as to read it is, in some respects, a mark of its influence. It did not have to be studied, or interrogated, it was simply *there*. It could be adapted, bowdlerised, reworked, and pirated and still not lose its authenticating sheen. It could be updated to take account of political and social developments unknown to its creator, but retain the animating spirit that had made it worth updating in the first place. Film historians have noted the comparative ease with which later adaptors managed to locate their treatments in landscapes that would have been familiar to contemporary audiences while remaining true to the mental atmosphere of the original. A second BBC version from 1965 opens with shots of a soldier driving across a nuclear minefield and an army general ordering an atomic strike. Airstrip One has metamorphosed into 'Pad Three', while the song of the prole woman in her dingy backyard has been transformed from a number that could have been sung on an interwar variety hall stage

("Twas only an 'opeless fancy') into a full-blown pop ballad. To the rear of a stage crowded out by Winston, Julia, and O'Brien lurk such classic Sixties preoccupations as the anti-nuclear Aldermaston marches and the scent of Swinging London.

This cannibalising tendency is even more marked in what might be called *Nineteen Eighty-Four*'s iconography, the development over the decades since first publication of its cover art. The inaugural UK paperback, published in 1954, appeared in the identikit Penguin fiction format, with the title printed in black on a white background sandwiched between two orange panels. In many ways the austerity of this standardised design was highly appropriate for a novel conceived in a world of rationing and paper shortages: Orwell, you feel, would have approved of its no-frills packaging, its modest canvassing of the book's merits, and the paperback publisher's customary assurance to the reader that the work is 'complete and unabridged'. But Penguin was a top-of-the-range imprint, over whose early productions hung an unmistakable air of uplift. By contrast, the US Signet edition of the early 1950s belongs to the American pulp tradition of bright colours, clamorous shout lines, sex, and violence. 'A strange view of life in 1984' shrieks the caption. 'Forbidden love . . . Fear . . . Betrayal'. Foregrounded beneath the shimmering outlines of the Ministry of Love are three deeply incongruous figures. Julia, stage right, is a muscular, leather-jacketed broad from the Bronx showing vast amounts of cleavage. Winston, seen in profile, and bearing a faint resemblance to Rock Hudson, looks as if he has just walked off the set of *West Side Story*. Behind them is a masked gorilla, who appears to be the custodian of a medieval torture chamber. Big Brother, whose features appear on an adjoining wall, is a caricature of Stalin with orc ears to match.

All the same, the sum of the Signet paperback is much more than its individual parts. In a single six-by-four-inch cover illustration it manages to locate *Nineteen Eighty-Four* in a defiantly inclusive context that includes popular science-fiction, classic American tough-guy naturalism, and anti-Soviet propagandising. Subsequent UK paperback jackets, on the other hand—fifteen of them in the past half-century—have preferred to concentrate on particular aspects of the Oceanian landscape, often to highly suggestive effect. The 1962 cover, for example, shows a single, lidless eye glaring from what looks like the heart of a labyrinth. The eye could be Big Brother's, staring from a poster or a television screen, but it might equally well be Winston's peering anxiously out at the rat cage. By the time of the 1966 reissue, on the other hand, Penguin had opted for a William Roberts painting of wartime bureaucratic routine, in which office workers lounge over their desks and answer telephones, with no hint of the terrors which life at the Ministry of Truth conceals. Another redesign, from 1999, moves off to a completely different coign of vantage by reproducing C.R.W. Nevinson's *The Soul of the Soulless City* (1920), a view of an imaginary part of the elevated Manhattan railway. Here cubist, futurist, and modernist techniques combine to produce something that while very nearly abstract doubles up as a clever piece of retro-forwarding: here in the late 1990s the date on the title page is already a decade and a half gone, but Nevinson's swooping cityscape has the effect of re-establishing it in a dizzyingly high-rise urban future.

IF THE VISUAL REIMAGINING of *Nineteen Eighty-Four* had to wait until the 1960s, then its critical reinterpretation had begun several years before. The first Orwell symposium, which occupied sixty or so pages of the *World Review*, dates from as early as June 1950: it included a puzzled attempt by the critic Herbert Read to understand the novel's 'strange success' ('Millions of people have read this book. Why? It had no charm; it makes no concession to sentiment. It is true that there are some traces of eroticism, but surely not enough to make the book, for those who like that sort of thing, a worthwhile experience') and a somewhat self-regarding note by Aldous Huxley, who maintained that advances in microphone technology would usher in an era of state-sponsored surveillance that Orwell could only have dreamed of. 'It looks very much as though the systematic brutality described in 1984 will seem to the really intelligent dictators of the future altogether too inefficient, messy and wasteful', Huxley brightly concluded. Subsequently, this first exegetical drip soon became an unstoppable tide. At least half a dozen critical studies had appeared by the end of the 1950s, nearly all of them convinced that, as Read put it, 'Orwell's last work will undoubtedly rank as his greatest'.

On the other hand, critics—*literary* critics, that is—were very often in two minds about the exact merits of *Nineteen Eighty-Four*. It was not only Herbert Read who wondered why a work that made so few concessions to what readers generally expected of a novel should have made so much of a hit. The suspicion that here was a mind at the end of its leash, and that sheer physical trauma involved in writing it had produced a detrimental aesthetic effect, was sometimes a little too flagrant to be gainsaid: Orwell's influence on the generation of writers who followed him was more likely to be detected in his essays or in the humanistic detail of a pre-war novel like *Coming Up for Air*. When a critic

sat down to examine the world of Oceania and the Two Minutes Hate in the twenty years after Orwell's death, he—and it was
mostly 'he'—tended to take his cue from the prevailing political
atmosphere. Thus, Gilbert Phelps, writing in 1961, at a time when
relations between the Soviet Union and the West were marginally
less strained than in the era of Truman and Stalin, straightaway
marks the novel down as a product of its time, from which the
gloss has already begun to flake away. It is surely by now apparent, Phelps insists, that

> a good deal of the excitement it aroused when it was
> first published (in 1949) was related to Cold War
> fever. Although it can still produce its *frissons* of hor-
> ror, the writing is frequently slack and tired compared
> to that of Orwell's earlier books . . . the tone is fre-
> quently shrill and hysterical, and the characterisation
> notably wooden.

To George Woodcock, alternatively, writing in the much more
politically charged atmosphere of 1967, four years after Kennedy's
assassination, with the Vietnam War in full swing and the democracies of Europe ever more conscious of the cold winds sweeping
in from the ground-down East, *Nineteen Eighty-Four*'s great merit
is that the book, and its author, have attracted 'the most hetero-
geneous following a writer can ever have accumulated'. British
Conservatives and free marketeers; American supporters of the
defeated 1964 Republican presidential candidate Barry Gold-
water and his adopted heir, the recently elected Governor of California, Ronald Reagan; anarchists who applauded a wholesale
demolition of the Marxist view of the state; 'middle-of-the-way'

left-wingers who worried over the threat posed by a centralised political system with individual liberty; disillusioned liberals in university humanities faculties made anxious by attacks on freedom of speech: each of these variegated constituencies found something in Winston Smith's vain attempt to throw off the shackles that bind him that a critic more absorbed by the 'slackness' of some of the figurative writing may occasionally miss.

As ever, it was the prophetic note that allowed Orwell to succeed where other dystopians had failed. The Marxist critic Raymond Williams, writing four years after Woodcock, is charmed by Orwell's foresight, keen on his 'liberating consciousness', impressed by 'The Principles of Newspeak' and its 'central perception' that there is a relationship between linguistic and social forms. To Williams, many of the Newspeak words—*prolefeed, speedwise, sexcrime*—already have an ominously familiar sound; much of the jargon promulgated by government departments in the modernising programmes of the 1960s 'is almost wholly Newspeak'. As for the obfuscations of news management and collective brainwashing which Orwell pioneers, 'the Fiction Department, as an institution, would now hardly be noticed'. When Winston describes the film-show pictures of aerial bombing, of boats exploding into matchwood and human limbs whirling into the air, 'it is as if he had seen the news reels from Vietnam'. Meanwhile, 'Big Brother is Watching You' has made its way into ordinary language as a metaphor for the surveillance techniques practised even by the democracies of the West. As an intransigent enemy of thoughtcrime and doublethink in a world where both these abstractions are palpably on the rise, 'Orwell is still very close and alive'.

And yet most of Williams's enthusiasm for *Nineteen Eighty-Four* is, in the end, deceptive or perhaps only disingenuous. As a

Marxist, he can never quite forgive Orwell for taking his model from Soviet Communism, or for creating—however unthinkingly—a propaganda tool that could be used by parties of the Right. He convicts Orwell—twenty years after his death—of a failure to understand that the post-war capitalist world of militarism and big corporations might end up looking 'very much like his projected Party'. And there are the proles, to Williams an eternally condescended to apathetic mass, treated by their creator with what is written off as 'stale revolutionary romanticism'. This, he concludes, is a world of one-dimensional situations where the 'ordinary resources of personal life' barely exist. 'It is strange that Orwell could oppose the controls and perversions with nothing better than the casual affair between Winston and Julia'. Which is, perhaps, Orwell's point—that a fugitive, opportunistic affair between two ill-matched lovers, one of whom is very probably an agent provocateur, is about the only form of dissension that a totalitarian state allows.

8. NEARING THE SELL-BY DATE

WHAT THE CRITIC Raymond Williams really thought about *Nineteen Eighty-Four*, as opposed to what he considered suitable for a mass-market primer aimed at university students, may be divined from a 1979 interview he gave to the Marxist *New Left Review*. This included a claim, advanced by the magazine's editors, that the novel 'will be a curio in 1984'. In contrast, most of the intellectual debate that surrounded the book at the time Williams was writing fastened onto the matter of its prescience, its absolute centrality to the events unfolding outside the window: the clock was ticking; who knew what among the horrors it described might be waiting when the ticking ceased. As the critic Christopher Small put it, from the vantage point of 1975, 'Already something like a count-down has started, and as the date with its imaginary horrors draws nearer, we feel an actual relief that events are not going according to plan'. Not that this meant, à la Williams, that Orwell became any less relevant merely because London had not been rechristened Airstrip One and radical gatherings broken up by the Thought Police. The date fascinates us, Small continues, and even if it was chosen arbitrarily out of a list that included 1980 and 1982, the knowledge scarcely diminishes 'the sinister power that this new Doomsday has over us'.

By the mid-1970s the date had begun to hang ominously over great areas of Anglo-American intellectual life, a spectral presence in book titles and works of political analysis. The musicologist Hans Keller, who had attended a music festival in Eastern Europe bedevilled by biased (i.e. pro-Communist) judging, was sufficiently enraged to call the collection of essays he published in 1977 *1975 (1984 Minus Nine)*. Anthony Burgess, who had enjoyed a fleeting acquaintanceship with Orwell in wartime Fitzrovia, produced his own English dystopia, *1985* (1978). As had been the case twenty years before, much of this enthusiasm was narrowly political. Just as, in the 1950s, Orwell had been taken up by the CIA in the service of world capitalism, so, in the mid-to-late 1970s, he was taken up by the British literary right in their attempts to confront what they regarded as the UK's flawed political and economic institutions. The period 1974–9 was a deeply demoralising time for the British body politic, characterised by minority governments, raging inflation, and industrial unrest. There was talk—vague talk, but talk nonetheless—of military takeovers. A television programme entitled *Who Says It Can Never Happen Here* featured a former government minister, Lord Chalfont, arguing that half the prerequisites for a society run in accordance with the Communist Manifesto were already in place.

Much of this was right-wing scaremongering, gleefully whipped up by Conservative-supporting newspapers. On the other hand, widespread resentment of the power supposedly wielded by trade unions reached boiling point in the 'Winter of Discontent' of 1978–9 when several million workers came out on strike, mountains of rubbish sacks lay uncollected in Trafalgar Square, and the leader of the London ambulancemen was quoted to the effect that 'if it means lives must be lost, that is how it must be'. To a novelist, or a polemicist, who burned to attack what was widely regarded as the spectacle of a Labour government being held to ransom by its union allies, *Nineteen Eighty-Four* was an infallible support. Its shadow hangs over Robert Moss's *The Collapse of Democracy* (1975), published to coincide with the launch of an influential right-wing faction called the National Association for Freedom, which opens with a fictitious letter from the London of 1985, now in a state of 'proto-Communism'. Half a decade later it was to stalk the margins of Julian Fane's novel *Revolution Island* (1980), which envisages a future of unbridled anarchy after 'our last Conservative government was deposed by the Trade Unions, over whom it had again attempted to assert its democratic authority'.

The single factor that unites most of the Orwell-inspired right-wing future-shock novels is their feebleness as pieces of fiction. There is no getting away from this. A bench-full of Booker Prize winners, intellectual polymaths, and one-time Communists who had seen the light scratched their heads over the political chaos of the 1970s, and the result is a novel like Kingsley Amis's *Russian Hide and Seek* (1980), set half a century after a Soviet takeover enabled by a breakdown in law and order ('There had been disorders here, runaway inflation, mass unemployment, strikes, strike-breaking, rioting, then much fiercer rioting when a leftist faction seized power'). At least one can say of *1985*, less than half of whose 240 pages are occupied by the novel itself, that Burgess intends seriously to engage with Orwell's ur-text: the opening sections offer a series of essays and mock interviews in which he addresses some of *Nineteen Eighty-Four*'s implications for the world of contemporary Britain. At the same time, in the wider context of international power politics, Burgess's objectives can look horribly localised, a file of domestic irritations that seismic shifts in the political landscape would rapidly sweep away.

How does Burgess's satirical view of the short-term future shape up? Beneath his broad-stroked brush, the British Isles have materialised into 'TUK' (The United Kingdom) humorously known as 'Tucland' (TUC is the acronym of the real-life Trades Union Congress), a fiefdom of organised labour where workers' rights are paramount, the closed shop relentlessly enforced, and dissenting voices routinely suppressed. Similar developments appear to be taking place across the Atlantic (the USA is jokingly referred to as 'Unhappy Syndicalized America'). Educational standards have collapsed—one of Burgess's better jokes involves the 'kumina' street gangs whose idea of adolescent rebellion is to converse in Latin and Greek—and, in a nod to the simplifications of Newspeak, the citizens are bidden to speak in 'WE' (Workers' English), an illiterate demotic in which 'You was' replaces 'You were'. In place of Big Brother, public spaces are decorated with portraits of 'Bill, the symbolic worker', a figurative reminder of the dignity of labour.

The rebellion of Bev Jones, Burgess's hero, whose wife has died in a blaze at a local hospital which the fire brigade had refused to extinguish, consists of tearing up his union card. This, as the government officials to whom he applies not unsympathetically explain, has the effect of rendering him unemployable. The 'freedom' he craves is, he is assured, merely a reactionary dream, 'Freedom to starve, freedom to be exploited'. As for any democratic rights he may or may not possess, it is left to his MP to point out that the word 'Socialist' or 'Conservative' no longer have any meaning: the workers run the country and they can do as they choose. Like Winston, Bev is taken off to be re-educated at a TUC rehabilitation centre in the country. The same Orwellian shadings can be detected in *Russian Hide and Seek*, set in the twenty-first century, fifty years after the 'Pacification'. Here, the UK has reverted to a curious semi-rural state—a car is a luxury item—bossed by a Russian aristocracy that is trying to restore a native culture more or less extinguished at the time of the invasion. As in *Nineteen Eighty-Four*, a worker ant—in this case a young officer named Petrovsky—decides to rebel, is encouraged by a colleague to join 'The Conspiracy' bent on overthrowing the ruling oligarchy, discovers that his fellow plotters are mostly double agents bent on sniffing out heresy, and is shot dead.

Although written amid the chaos of 1978–9, which underpins Amis's account of the circumstances in which the 'Pacification' takes place, *Russian Hide and Seek* was not published until 1980. By this time Britain had a new prime minister, Margaret Thatcher, to whom, at a Downing Street reception, Amis presented a copy. Learning of the novel's theme, Mrs Thatcher is supposed to have remarked, 'Find another crystal ball'. Come the early 1980s, Anglo-American politics had turned sharply to the right. By the beginning of 1981, Reagan was in the White House. Detente had collapsed. A US boycott of the 1980 Moscow Olympics was followed by a Russian boycott of the 1984 Los Angeles games. The 'Star Wars' missile programme proceeded apace. It was in this febrile atmosphere that the countdown to 1984 reached its final stages. Western journalists who visited Moscow for the 1980 Games were instantly struck by the air of familiarity. Christopher Booker recalled how he and his colleagues had walked to the Olympic Lenin Stadium between two unbroken ranks of Soviet soldiers, while from every available wall giant-sized posters of Leonid Brezhnev proclaimed the single word 'Peace!'

Once again the American media were determined to enlist Orwell as an anti-Communist prophet. If Walter Cronkite's hour-long CBS special *1984 Revisited* (broadcast in June 1983) was reasonably objective—the computerised 'face' of Big Brother mingles the physiognomies of Hitler, Stalin, Mussolini, Mao, and the West's current bogeyman, the Ayatollah Khomeini—then the neo-Conservative Norman Podhoretz was in no doubt where he stood. Under the heading 'If Orwell Were Alive Today', he informed readers of *Harper's* magazine that, were the author of *Nineteen Eighty-Four* still on the planet, he would be lining up to defend freedom with William F. Buckley Jr. and Henry Kissinger. Meanwhile, the Western world's keen interest in what a man a third of a century dead could tell it about the 1980s was confirmed by Orwell's appearance on the cover of *Time* magazine, late in November 1983.

It had always been assumed that the novel would merit a big-budget movie to be released in the year of its setting. The chief difficulty, a third of a century after Orwell's death, was to establish who now owned the rights. They turned out to belong to the American producer Marvin Rosenblum, who, together with the British director Michael Radford, and with funding from Richard Branson's Virgin group, began work towards the end of 1983. Anxious to procure Hollywood A-listers for the major parts, Rosenblum tried to persuade Jamie Lee Curtis to play Julia and Marlon Brando to impersonate O'Brien, but had to settle for Suzanna Hamilton and the ailing Richard Burton. As for establishing a cinematic first principle, the contract Rosenblum had agreed with Sonia Brownell shortly before her death in 1980 had come down firmly on the side of realism by specifying that 'the purchaser will make good faith efforts not to make the picture in the *Star Wars* or *2001: A Space Odyssey* genre of science fiction'. All this gives *Nineteen Eighty-Four*, mostly filmed on location in London and including shots of the Ministry of Truth's original, the University of London Senate House, a distinctly period feel: Radford and his cinematographer Roger Deakins are supposed to have wanted to film it in black and white. John Hurt, as Winston, wandering around the bomb-cratered streets or labouring up the stone staircase of Victory Mansions, could almost be a refugee from the Blitz. This suspicion is reinforced by the newsreel footage of collapsing buildings and firestorms beamed out to patriotic cinema audiences, which looks as if it uses wartime images.

Elsewhere, the film carefully abstracts its symbolism from a number of bygone tyrannies. Radford's first wife, Czechoslovakian by birth, had been enrolled as a Young Pioneer. Parsons's daughter, standing vigilantly by the door of her apartment in her Junior Spy uniform as Winston crawls home from the Ministry of Truth, is clearly modelled on this template. The posters on Winston's wall are parodies of Soviet propaganda literature. Alternatively, the open-sided trucks bringing the guilty to be publicly hanged in Victory Square are uncomfortably close to Second World War–era photographs of Nazi lorries taking Jewish prisoners away to the death camps. This complex chain of derivation was one of the film's strengths. So, too, were some of the individual performances. John Hurt, then only a year or so older than his alter ego, looks half-starved: he maintained, not wholly humorously, that there were resemblances between Winston's plight and his own upbringing as the son of a Humberside clergyman. Burton, who had demanded that his boiler suit should be hand-stitched by a Savile Row tailor, is grave and sacerdotal, willing Winston to trust him, offering glasses of wine and hope with a half-benevolent stare.

Nineteen Eighty-Four premiered in London on 7 October 1984. While respectfully received by the critics, it was not a commercial success: the $8.4 million (£6.8 million) its distributors, Twentieth Century Fox, took at the box office scarcely balanced the £5.5 million ($6.8 million) it had cost to film. In this context, it is tempting to claim that Orwell's most far-reaching on-screen impact came by way of a television commercial to launch the Apple Macintosh home computer whose main airing took place during Super Bowl XVIII on 22 January 1984. A pet project of the Apple co-founder Steve Jobs, and as such pressed by him on a less than enthusiastic board, Ridley Scott's minute-long ad starts with a procession of cowed, boiler-suited drones marching through a tunnel lined with surveillance screens. As they sit attending to one of Big Brother's harangues on a giant screen, a muscular blonde woman, wearing red shorts and a white tank top with a cartoon silhouette of an Apple computer and clutching a sledgehammer, dashes into the room with the Thought Police in vengeful pursuit. Just as Big Brother is assuring his audience that 'We Shall Prevail', she hurls her weapon at his image. In the earth-shattering explosion that follows, the audience seem frozen into petrified stasis. The accompanying text reads: 'On January 24th, Apple Computer will introduce Macintosh. And you'll see why 1984 won't be like "1984"'. After threats of a lawsuit by the filmmakers, there were no further showings, but sales of Apple Macs reached $150 million in the first three months of distribution.

AFTER SEVERAL FALSE STARTS, legal manoeuvres, and the retention of a fair amount of Dominic Muldowney's original score, a soundtrack to Radford's film was eventually recorded by the Eurythmics, a British synth-pop duo whose 'Sexcrime (Nineteen Eighty-Four)' was a top-five hit on the UK singles chart in December 1984. But pop music's engagement with the novel dates back to the late 1960s. Indeed, it might be said that almost from the moment that pop started to take itself seriously, and when the pop lyrics came to be studied in isolation from the music that accompanied them, it began to take a serious interest in Orwell. This is particularly evident in the music that emanated from the American West Coast in the period 1967–70, much of whose subtext takes in denunciations of the heavy-handed tactics of local police departments—the LAPD in particular—in monitoring the activities of nascent hippy communities. Spirit's single '1984', issued in early 1970, and considered too controversial for radio play, draws a parallel between the eavesdropping of the telescreen and police surveillance helicopters. Nineteen eighty-four is 'knocking at your door', the band's singer, Randy California, intones. 'Will you let it come? Will you let it ruin your life?' Someone will be waiting in the shadows, 'And yes, he's gonna tell you darkness gives you much more than you get from the light'.

'The Red Telephone' on Love's *Forever Changes* album (1968) is a response to the Sunset Strip riots that took place in Los Angeles late in 1966 ('They're locking them up today / They're throwing away the key / I wonder who it'll be tomorrow, you or me?'). Even satirical treatments of hippy-dom and the West Coast counterculture—see *We're Only in It for the Money* (1968) by Frank Zappa and the Mothers of Invention—start from a position that is, in itself, Orwellian: that American youth are being brainwashed by an authoritarian consumer culture designed to replace genuine freedom with a state-sanctioned conformity.

And in popular music, as in literature, the clock was beginning to tick. 'Revolt into Style' (1979), a complaint about the retrogressive cultural tendencies of the era by the British singer-songwriter Bill Nelson, notes that 'though the time is nearly 1984, it feels like 1965'. A feature of the musical scene from the early Seventies onward is the number of *Nineteen Eighty-Four*–inspired concept albums: the jazz-rock bassist Hugh Hopper's in 1973; the former Genesis guitarist Anthony Phillips's in 1981; the one-time Yes keyboard player Rick Wakeman's in the same year. The Hopper and Phillips albums are instrumentals, with little direct connection to Orwell's text. Hopper remarked that 'there's nothing specific about the book because I hate parallels between media— music is one thing and literature another', although his dreamy, tape-looped soundscapes are named after Oceania's four state ministries, Miniluv, Minipax, Minitrue, and Miniplenty. Wakeman, alternatively, produced a full-blown song-suite, with lyrics by Tim Rice, the effect only slightly dissipated by his admission that some of the contents had a more personal context. 'Julia', in particular, was dedicated to his wife.

Yet the novel's most committed pop-world fan in the Seventies and the decades that followed was David Bowie. Fans of *The Rise and Fall of Ziggy Stardust and the Spiders from Mars* (1972) and *Aladdin Sane* (1973) had already noted his interest in ravaged cityscapes and futuristic alienation. In fact, the Orwell fixation in his work goes back at least as far as the highly dystopian 'Cygnet Committee' from *David Bowie* (1969), with its lines about 'And we can force you to be free / And we can force you to believe' and the narrator's confession that 'I once read a book in which the lovers were slain / For they knew not the words of the Free

States' refrain'. By late 1973, with the covers album *Pin-ups* in the can, he had a much more ambitious scheme in mind: nothing less than a stage musical of *Nineteen Eighty-Four*, for which he would write the songs. In the event, after a certain amount of negotiation with the Orwell Estate (Sonia was apparently horrified), permission was refused, but the material—'We Are the Dead', 'Big Brother', '1984' ('Beware the ravening jaw of 1984')—resurfaced on the second side of 1974's *Diamond Dogs*. Bowie's interest in totalitarianism kept up. In 1976, he remarked that Hitler was 'the first rock star' and, on arriving at London's Victoria Station, was alleged to have given the Nazi salute to a crowd of waiting fans. There was talk of his producing 'organic music'—whatever that meant—for Michael Radford's film, and as late as the 1990s he proposed, again unsuccessfully, that the Estate should authorise an Orwell biopic with himself in the title role.

Meanwhile the makers of the new brands of punk and New Wave music blasting out of London, New York, and Los Angeles were claiming Orwell as a natural ally. Here in the era of renaissant Conservatism, Reagan, Thatcher, the Falklands War, and (in the UK at least) three million unemployed, the author of *Nineteen Eighty-Four* seemed more pertinent than ever—someone who, were he still alive, could be relied upon to 'lay into the Thatcher gang', as a writer on the *New Musical Express* once put it, and expose the authoritarian tendencies of the modern state ('Here come the police / in 1984' as the Clash sang in '1977'). The lyrics of Elvis Costello's 'Night Rally', from the album *This Year's Model* (1978), read like reportage from Victory Square: the 'corporation logo' is flashing on and off in the sky, and names are being logged 'in the forbidden book'.

The same eagerness to acknowledge influence was true of America, where a verse of the Dead Kennedys' 1979 single 'California Über Alles' opens with the line 'Now it is 1984' and goes on to excoriate the then Governor of California, Jerry Brown, on the assumption that, at the end of his gubernatorial term, he would stand for the presidency in 1984 with the aim of extirpating every liberal freedom currently on offer.

Much of pop's absorption in *Nineteen Eighty-Four* was no more than name-checking, a kind of generalised distaste for authority, surveillance, and news management—each recognisably present on both sides of the Iron Curtain—finding a symbolic point of focus. Here and there, though, comes evidence of a more sustained engagement with the novel and, in particular, an interest in elements of it that exist beyond, or in opposition to, the atmosphere of Two Minute Hates, the manipulation of language, and the terrors of Room 101. The British singer-songwriter Paul Weller, for example, then a motivating force behind the Jam, first refers to the novel in 'Standards', a track from the band's second album, *This Is the Modern World* (1977). The song itself is a conventional and slightly unfocused assault on the state machine that grinds its operatives down ('We make the standards and we make the rules / And if you don't abide by them you must be a fool'), but the banality of the material is redeemed by the distinctly Orwellian final couplet: 'And ignorance is strength, we have God on our side / Look, you know what happened to Winston'. Even more suggestive, perhaps, is 'Tales from the Riverbank', a B-side from 1981, and a paean to the Surrey countryside in which Weller had roamed as a child: 'No fears to worry in this golden country / Woke at sunrise, went home at sunset'.

Pastoralism in English pop music goes back to Pink Floyd's *The Piper at the Gates of Dawn* (1967), if not beyond it. Here, though, Weller is framing it in the context of Winston's dream of rural safety, the kind of security he feels, however temporarily, in his encounters with Julia in an English countryside where, even now, there are no surveillance cameras and the Thought Police seldom stray.

9. THE POST-TRUTH WORLD

IN THE LAST MONTHS of the twentieth century, somewhat to his own surprise, the writer Christopher Hitchens managed to procure a visa for the Democratic People's Republic of Korea. By this time 'The Great Leader', Kim Il Sung, was dead, although his portrait was still displayed on every public building. All other senior posts were occupied by 'The Dear Leader', his son, Kim Jong Il. Over the course of his visit, Hitchens—who seems to have been alternately intrigued and horrified—kept a record of the countless ways in which public life in North Korea might be thought to mirror the arrangements in Oceania. Among other expressions of confidence in the regime, he observed the spectacle of children marching to school in formation singing uplifting songs. Lapel buttons embossed with the Dear Leader's features were mandatory. Loudspeakers and radios broadcast an endless stream of propaganda. On a permanent war footing; contemptuous of foreigners and foreign military power; and obsessed with mass sports, mass exercise, and communal activity generally, Kim Jong Il's fiefdom prohibited all news from beyond its borders and any contact with other countries. A labyrinth of tunnels beneath the capital city, Pyongyang, connected the various repressive organs of the state. Other features of life in North Korea included newspapers with no news, shops with no goods, and an airport with almost no planes on its runways.

There was only one way in which the country fell short of the conditions described in *Nineteen Eighty-Four*, and this was its insufficient grasp of the advantages of surveillance technology: though punitive and overbearing, the regime was simply too impoverished and cack-handed to insist on telescreens or even the mass distribution of radio sets. On the other hand, in the matter of limiting, if not extinguishing, individual freedoms, the brand of repressiveness on offer in North Korea had moved even further than the proscriptions of Oceania. Winston and Julia would have no chance at all for a moment of private life in the countryside or anywhere else, Hitchens believed. Elsewhere, like a stack of paperclips obeying the magnet's call, pieces of authentic Orwell detail continued to pile up: the 'hate' sessions staged at factories and offices; a games evening at which Hitchens was shown flashcards of an enemy soldier speeding towards him, only to be replaced by the shining face of the Great Leader. This, he concluded, was a society in which individual life was *absolutely pointless*, where everything that was not compulsory was routinely suppressed. The resulting misery was indescribable 'without reference to a certain short novel that had been bashed out on an old typewriter, against the clock, by a dying English radical half a century before'.

ORWELL'S NOVEL HAD BEEN INTENDED, in its author's words, as a 'warning' rather than a prophecy. It was tempting to assume that the post-1989 collapse of the Soviet Union and its satellites and the political reconfiguration of Eastern Europe had rendered the warning obsolete. If state socialism had been seen to have failed, then surely the propaganda weapons that had exposed it would follow the same road to superannuation? World literature is littered with the bones of eye-catching dystopias acclaimed as works of extraordinary prescience in their day that are now no more than period curios. After all, who reads *When the Sleeper Wakes* or *The Secret of the League* in 2019? On the contrary, *Nineteen Eighty-Four* continued to embed itself in popular culture. Though the proliferation of international editions makes overall computation difficult, world sales in the last decade of the twentieth century and the first decade of the twenty-first are thought to have risen to 40 million copies. The novel became a staple of school curricula and examination syllabi. Television reinvented it for non-Orwellian purposes (*Room 101*, *Big Brother*) and the satire of which it consists was inevitably subjected to pastiche—see, for example, Matt Nix's short film *Me and the Big Guy* (1999), whose protagonist relishes his daily exposure to Oceania's leader to the point of regularly hobnobbing with him. There was a rash of stage dramatizations, radio plays, even an opera by Lorin Maazel, which premiered in 2005 and featured a herd-like chorus in perpetual transit across a spotlight-strafed stage. If Michael Radford's *Nineteen Eighty-Four* was the last authentic wide-screen treatment, then countless other films have referenced it or borrowed from its atmospherics: Terry Gilliam's *Brazil* (1985), filmed only a month or so later, even made use of some of Radford's sets.

The crucial factor, in all of this, was the novel's versatility, its continuing relevance to a world that Orwell had no way of foreseeing. As time moved on, then so did the prism through which critics—and ordinary readers—tended to regard it. While Soviet-style economic centralism had been and gone, there were plenty of other authoritarian regimes whose disregard for individual autonomy seemed even worse. The journalist Emma Larkin, touring Burma in the early 2000s, reported that there was a joke that Orwell had actually written three novels about the country: *Burmese Days*, *Animal Farm*, and *Nineteen Eighty-Four*. Twenty years after Hitchens's visit, journalists who finesse their way into North Korea by joining the state-supervised tourist caravans bring back reports of traffic-less streets arbitrarily closed off to facilitate rehearsals for mass rallies, dioramas of the Korean War that fail to mention the involvement of the Russians and the Chinese, 'hundred-day pushes' when everybody is expected to work extra hours in factory or office and attend extra political classes, and—if the reporter is exceptionally pertinacious—the terrible squalor of the landscapes beyond the tourist zones, where sewage runs down open drains in the middle of the streets and the houses are made of unpainted breezeblocks.

In the meantime, Orwell's status as a kind of moral litmus paper ripe for dipping into some of the foetid ethical waters of the modern age meant that *Nineteen Eighty-Four* was always likely to be pressed into service whenever a great liberal cause seemed to be threatened by ideology or a disregard for objective truth. Certainly its shadow hung over one of the great intellectual rows of the 1990s. This was the Sokal Hoax, named after the New York University physics professor who submitted a contribution to *Social Text*, a journal of postmodern cultural studies, entitled 'Transgressing the Boundaries: Towards a Transformative Hermeneutics of Quantum Gravity'. Sokal's article, a parody intended to expose what he regarded as the magazine's unquestioning 'progressive' agenda, its lack of peer review, and the deconstructionist philosophy that influenced its editorial politics, contained the incredible (and unchallenged) statement that 'it is becoming increasingly apparent that physical "reality" is fundamentally a social and linguistic construct'. What was needed was an 'emancipatory mathematics' that would undermine the prescriptions of 'elite science'. It was useless for the editors to complain that Sokal had misunderstood deconstructionism, or that the way in which scientists approach their work is at least indirectly influenced by the political systems of which they are a part: most critics concluded that the journal's editorial stance was a deliberate, Orwellian attempt to undermine observable fact in pursuit of a political agenda.

As ever, it depended on what you meant by 'Orwellian', an adjective that, here in the early twenty-first century, has a variety of individual, though sometimes complementary meanings. North Korea, for example, fits the bill by dint of its all-round repressiveness, its determination to suppress any individual instincts that its citizens may possess simply as a political principle. Much more common, in the world of Google and Facebook, is its application to intrusive technology: CCTV cameras on every street corner; data-harvesting; online profiling; the Chinese surveillance and artificial intelligence system that reduces the status of its citizenry to that of a mass of endlessly scrutinised worker ants—all these, the argument runs, and however benignly or at any rate commercially conceived, are Orwellian, for their aim is to capture individual lives in a net thrown out by some higher corporate or governmental power. Finally, there is the suspicion that *Nineteen Eighty-Four* is at its most prophetic—and at its most sinister—in the field of language and the uses to which it can be put in the battle to undermine objective truth.

This tendency is a feature of almost every brand of western politics. In December 2018, when the UK parliament's deliberations about Brexit had reached crisis point, the Conservative MP Sir Bernard Jenkin declared that the situation in which he found himself was 'Orwellian'. It turned out that Jenkin was reacting to a claim by one of his fellow Tory MPs that his hostility to the Prime Minister's proposed Brexit deal was 'treasonable'. How could this be treasonable, Jenkin wondered. By agreeing to the deal as it now stood, Britain would not be properly detaching itself from Europe. And yet a majority of British citizens had voted in a referendum to leave the EU, and the Conservative government that had taken office after the General Election of 2017 had included in its manifesto a commitment to recognise the referendum result. Sir Bernard could be accused of pig-headedness, or obstruction, or an obstinate refusal to compromise, but it was difficult to believe that what he had done amounted to 'treason' either to his country, his party leader, or anyone else. The admittedly adversarial position in which he stood was being undermined by the disingenuous use of language.

And language, one feels, lies at the heart of the most recent 'Orwellian' moment in international affairs—the discovery that in the weeks following the Trump inauguration, sales of *Nineteen Eighty-Four* in the United States had risen by an estimated 950 per cent. But what real connection does the world of Oceania, Two Minutes Hate, and telescreens have to Donald Trump? Since that fateful day on Capitol Hill more than one symposium has been convened to debate the President's undeniable authoritarian tendencies or pose the question 'Is Trump a Fascist?' but there is a limit to how far you can go with inquiries of this sort. Orwell himself admitted—as long ago as 1944—that the word had lost any meaning it might once have possessed. And while Trump may be illiberal, spiteful, reactionary, vainglorious, crony-haunted, and xenophobic—all qualities which bygone Fascist leaders possessed in abundance—he altogether lacks what may be regarded as the authenticating mark of any self-respecting authoritarian regime: the ability of its leader to control his executive. In place of some self-sustaining cadre with an almost mythological belief in its own virtue and the destiny it is divinely appointed to fulfil, there is only opportunism, expediency, backbiting, and chaos.

Much closer to the world of *Nineteen Eighty-Four*, though, is what might be called the alternative-reality aspect of much modern American life. Strictly speaking, this is pre-Trump in origin. During the days of George W. Bush's presidency, the American journalist Ron Suskind ran into a White House official who criticised him for living in what he called the 'reality-based community'. 'That's not the way the world really works any more', Suskind was briskly informed. 'We make our own reality'. The first signs that the Trump administration might be fashioning its own reality came in the row that followed the inauguration, when the incoming presidential press secretary, Sean Spicer, spectacularly lost his temper with a group of journalists keen to compare the precise number of spectators who had attended the ceremony with the significantly larger group of anti-Trump protestors who had arrived in Washington on the day afterwards. This, Spicer declared, was 'deliberate false reporting'. He also declared that the pro-Trumpers constituted the largest group of people ever assembled for an inauguration. Crowd estimation is an inexact science, but photographic evidence that Obama's inauguration attracted more supporters than his successor's was incontestable. Here the Trump administration appeared to be performing the classic Orwellian trick of trying to render an obvious lie believable.

It was left to the President's adviser Kellyanne Conway, stung by incontrovertible evidence that more Americans were keener on complaining about her newly elected boss than supporting him, to declare that Spicer hadn't lied in claiming that Trump-ites had outnumbered protestors: he was offering 'alternative facts'. Naturally, in producing this defence, Ms Conway had her supporters. She was a PR person, we were told, operating in a world where all values are expedient and abstract nouns like 'liberal' and 'democracy' can undergo 180-degree turns without the people perverting their original definitions even knowing that the trick has been played. Even so, there was no getting away with the words she uttered—'alternative facts', a phrase as bizarre and implausible as 'benevolent dictator' or 'God-fearing atheist', and betraying, along the way, the fact that the person who minted it has no idea of how language works or how it should be treated by people who want to communicate by using it.

The first two years of the Trump administration brought almost weekly examples of 'alternative facts'. CNN, for example, once screened a caption that ran 'White House denies Trump was mocking Kavanaugh accuser after Trump mocks Kavanaugh accuser'. In some ways it might even be argued that the process refines on Orwell's original. Big Brother, after all, brought a certain amount of guile to pretending that what he said was true: a reduction of the quantity of rationed goods available to Oceania's cowed citizenry was always described as a 'readjustment', which is sleight of hand but not technically a lie. If the Trump White House is brought incontrovertible proof of something it would prefer not to have happened, then it simply denies it while impugning the integrity of the person or the institution that exposed it. In the wake of yet another devastating hurricane season, and a series of

Californian summers ruined by smog, the climate can always be described as 'glorious' if President Trump sees it that way.

All this is naturally made easier by the emergence of two binary information systems in the United States, one which supports nearly every task the president embarks on and the other which routinely disparages it. It has several times been pointed out by concerned media analysts that, as an old BBC hand recently put it, Fox News's agenda-setting power relies on the creation of a solitary information system in which true believers get all their news from a single, uncontested point of view. Any news that might seem to contradict it is merely an alternative fact, at best inaccurate, at worst toxic alien matter malignly insinuated in the wellspring of truth. As for the cumulative effect, it is not, perhaps, that the hundreds of thousands of people who went out to buy copies of *Nineteen Eighty-Four* and propelled it to the top of the Amazon chart in the week that Trump assumed office thought that he had the potential to be a Fascist dictator, or that some democratic barricade had been breached (although he lost the popular vote, Trump won the election according to the rules. His victory was far less obviously corrupt than, say, that of the ballot box–stuffing Lyndon Johnson in 1964). Rather it was that his ascent to the leadership of the western world, with its hints of Russian interference, its social media subterfuge, its general bad fellowship, and its compromised motive, was taken as a symbol of everything that gone wrong with that world's moral compass.

What would Orwell have thought of 'alternative facts'? From his vantage point as the former employee of an organisation broadcasting propaganda to a South East Asia threatened by invasion, he would probably have pointed out that these obfuscations are not merely a by-blow of total war—for who could really complain about the RAF overstating the number of Nazi planes brought down in the Battle of Britain?—but a fundamental part of the way in which the contemporary autocrat and truth defiler faces up to the world. All this exemplifies not only the contemporary relevance of *Nineteen Eighty-Four*—not always a point in a novel's favour—but also the multiple, different constituencies to whom it appeals. To Orwell biographers, it is important for what it tells us about the man who wrote it and the fragments of personal history hidden beneath its surface. To a literature specialist, it is a genre-defining template for the dystopian novels of the past half-century, nearly all of which offer an alternative world with a quasi-religious sense of its own certainty (in the case of Margaret Atwood's *The Handmaid's Tale*, a genuine religious sense) opposed by a tiny cadre of conspiring ingrates.

To a psychologist, alternatively, it is a penetrating study of alienation. To an historian, meanwhile, it is, at bottom, a projection of the Second World War, many of whose incidental details can be tracked back to a specific event. Take, for example, the diary entry in which Winston records himself watching a propaganda film that shows a lifeboat full of refugees being bombed. Whether or not (as some critics suspect) this is a memento of the torpedoing of the *Struma* by Russian submarines in 1942 as it attempted to transport 800 Jews from Romania to Palestine, the clincher is the date—4 April, which just happens to be the anniversary of the foundation of the SS and the day on which Allied forces entered the Ohrdurf forced-labour camp and came face to face with the full enormity of the Holocaust. All of which perhaps ignores one of the most crucial background factors to any book, good or bad—the circumstances in which it was written. For it is impossible for anyone who knows only the faintest outline of

Orwell's life to read *Nineteen Eighty-Four* without thinking of a tall, spindly man in wretched health, smouldering cigarette in one hand, hunched over a typewriter in a stuffy, badly heated bedroom while outside the North Atlantic wind lashes against the windows and beneath him a small boy plays with his toys on the hearthrug.

And finally there is the question of Orwell's state of mind when he came to the end of this Herculean task—an endeavour, it is worth remembering, that had taken him five years to accomplish and whose last stretch may very well have helped to kill him. How did he feel when he laid down his pen? Critical orthodoxy suggests that he was at the end of his physical tether and that *Nineteen Eighty-Four*'s horrors are a direct consequence of an inner turmoil fed by his mortal illness. But his friend George Woodcock had another idea. Essentially the ordeal that Orwell put himself through to complete this final novel was cathartic, Woodcock thought. By writing about the terrors that obsessed him, he had got them out of his system. Now, curiously enough, he was at peace.

APPENDIX: THE MANUSCRIPT
OF *NINETEEN EIGHTY-FOUR*

AS HIS WIDOW, Sonia, later remarked, Orwell 'was not a very good manuscript keeper'. On a visit to Jura, shortly after his death, she discovered a pile of corrected typescript and handwritten pieces of paper in the bedroom where he had written the bulk of *Nineteen Eighty-Four*. Not unreasonably, she assumed that this was the manuscript from which he had typed up the finished version of the novel sent to Secker & Warburg at the end of 1948. The material was donated by her to a charity auction held in June 1952 and purchased by Scribner's of New York for the sum of £50 ($140). Scribner's subsequently resold it to a collector in Kansas for $275 (£98). In 1969 it was bought by Daniel G. Siegel for $5,000 (£2,093). The manuscript is now at Brown University.

Investigation showed the manuscript to be incomplete. In fact, only 40 per cent of the finished novel had survived. What remains can be divided into four sections: thirteen pages of the draft that Orwell worked on in the summer of 1946; nine pages from the 1947 redraft; a solitary page from the version typed up by Mrs Christen; and the remainder (by far the largest part) from Orwell's final rewrite in 1948. Much of the rewriting is extensive. As Siegel put it, 'The pages were nondescript, typed and handwritten in ink with pages and corrections in ink, with a great deal of over-writing on the typed pages'.

Most of the corrections show Orwell tightening up his prose, removing superfluous phrases, and taking out redundant expressions, but there are three more substantial passages that failed to appear in the finished version. One is a horrifying scene in the propaganda reel that Winston watches at the prole cinema involving the lynching of a negro woman and the desecration of her aborted child. Another is a description of the journey to O'Brien's apartment. Most interesting of all, in terms of the novel's denouement, is a scene in which Winston and Julia re-encounter each other after leaving O'Brien. Here Winston experiences 'a curious feeling that although the purpose for which she had waited was to arrange another meeting, the embrace she had given him was intended as some kind of good-bye'.

There are also several pieces of self-censorship. Thus 'an old fat Jew' trying to swim away from a pursuing helicopter in the propaganda film becomes 'a huge great fat man'. Similarly, the draft of Winston's interrogation at the Ministry of Love, where he is shown photographs of Julia and himself, is turned up a notch or two to include evidence 'of Julia & himself in the act of making love'. For further information, see Peter Davison, ed., *George Orwell: Nineteen Eighty-Four: The Facsimile of the Extant Manuscript: With a Preface by Daniel G. Siegel* (1984).

ACKNOWLEDGEMENTS

Extracts from Orwell's published works are reproduced with the kind permission of A.M. Heath Ltd.

I should particularly like to salute David Ryan, who allowed me to see an early copy of his recently published *George Orwell on Screen*. Warm thanks are also offered to Professor Peter Davison; Sarah Aitchison, Head of Special Collections at University College London; Georgie Kee; Bill Hamilton; Professor Jean Seaton; Gordon Wise; and Richard Blair.

NOTES AND FURTHER READING

There are five full-length biographies of Orwell, by Bernard Crick (1980 and revised editions), Michael Shelden (1991), Jeffrey Meyers (2000), Gordon Bowker (2003), and D.J. Taylor (2003). Each of them contains useful material on the writing of *Nineteen Eighty-Four*. Orwell's *Complete Works* have been edited in twenty volumes by Professor Peter Davison (1998). Of particular relevance are *Volume XV: Two Wasted Years: 1943*; *Volume XVI: I Have Tried to Tell the Truth: 1943–1944*; *Volume XVII: I Belong to the Left: 1945*; *Volume XVIII: Smothered Under Journalism: 1946*; *Volume XIX: It Is What I Think: 1947–1948*; *Volume XX: Our Job Is to Make Life Worth Living: 1949–1950*. See also Davison's supplementary volume, *The Lost Orwell* (2006).

Among recent critical studies, Christopher Hitchens, *Orwell's Victory* (2002, later editions are titled *Why Orwell Matters*); John Rodden, ed., *The Cambridge Companion to George Orwell* (2007); Robert Colls, *George Orwell: English Rebel* (2013); and David Dwan, *Liberty, Equality & Humbug: Orwell's Political Ideals*

(2018) are recommended. See also Dennis Glover's recent novelisation of Orwell's later life, *The Last Man in Europe* (2017). For a valuable psychological sketch of Orwell by a close friend, see Anthony Powell, *To Keep the Ball Rolling: Volume I: Infants of the Spring* (1976), 129–42.

1. THE TERRORS OF POWER

For a selection of reviews of *Nineteen Eighty-Four*, see Jeffrey Meyers, ed., *George Orwell: The Critical Heritage* (1975), 247–93. 'The book seems to have had a good reception', Orwell to Leonard Moore, 22 June 1949, Davison, ed., *Complete Works Volume XX*, 140. For Bernard Crick's comment, see 'Nineteen Eighty-Four: context and controversy', in Rodden, ed., *The Cambridge Companion to George Orwell*, 146. On the international political background, Jeremy Isaacs and Taylor Downing, *Cold War* (1998), 22–61.

Anthony Powell remembers visiting Orwell in hospital in October 1949 in *Infants of the Spring*, 141. The friend who saw him on Christmas afternoon 1949 was Malcolm Muggeridge.

2. LIFE INTO ART

'His imaginative powers, remarkable in one direction', Anthony Powell, *Miscellaneous Verdicts: Writings on Writers 1946–1989* (1990), 283. For his relationship with Jacintha Buddicom, see her *Eric and Us: A Remembrance of George Orwell* (1974, rev. edition 2006). Richard Rees remembers the conversation about seeing your name in print in *George Orwell: Fugitive from the Camp of Victory* (1961), 44.

For Orwell's pre-war reputation, Fredric Warburg, *An Occupation for Gentlemen* (1959), 231. 'If I should peg out in the next few years', Orwell to Richard Rees, 5 July 1946, *Complete Works Volume XVIII*, 340. Anthony Burgess writes about Orwell's fondness for 'rural' metaphors in *1985* (1978), 237. For 'Clink', see Davison, ed., *Complete Works Volume X: A Kind of Compulsion: 1903–1936*, 254–60. On Jack Bumstead, D.J. Taylor, 'He Put My Brother in His Book', in Mark Bostridge, ed., *Lives for Sale: Biographers' Tales* (2004), 177–80.

3. INFLUENCE AND INSPIRATION

'Why I Write' was originally published in *Gangrel*. See *Complete Works Volume XVIII*, 316–21. 'I don't understand or take any interest in politics', letter to Eleanor Jaques, 22 October 1931 [private collection]. 'Now that my book is published', letter to Eleanor, 15 January 1936 [private collection]. On Orwell in Wigan,

Colls, *English Rebel*, 55–6. The publisher who met him shortly before he went to Spain was Fred Warburg, *An Occupation for Gentlemen*, 231.

'But the thing that I saw in your face', lines taken from a poem beginning 'The Italian soldier shook my hand', which appears in the essay 'Looking Back on the Spanish War'. Davison, ed., *Complete Works Volume XIII: All Propaganda Is Lies*, 496–511. This originally appeared in the magazine *New Road* in 1943, but the exact date of composition is unknown. The Dos Passos letter is quoted in Powell, *Miscellaneous Verdicts*, 251.

Orwell's *Tribune* review of dystopian novels by Jack London, H.G. Wells, Aldous Huxley, and Ernest Bramah appeared in *Tribune* on 12 July 1940 and is reprinted in Davison, ed., *Complete Works Volume XII: A Patriot After All: 1940–1941*, 210–13. On Orwell's time at the BBC, W.J. West, *The Larger Evils: Nineteen Eighty-Four: The Truth Behind the Satire* (1992), 55–65; Desmond Avery, *George Orwell at the BBC in 1942* (2017). 'The Germans announce', diary entry of 11 June 1942, Davison ed., *All Propaganda Is Lies*, 355–6.

For his opinion of the BBC ('something halfway between a girls' school and a lunatic asylum'), diary entry of 14 March, 1942, *Complete Works Volume XIII*, 229. 'Two wasted years', letter to Philip Rahv, 9 December 1943, *Complete Works Volume XVI*, 22. The remarks about 'keeping our propaganda slightly less disgusting than it might otherwise have been' are contained in a letter to George Woodcock, 2 December 1942, *Complete Works Volume XIV: Keeping Our Little Corner Clean: 1942–1943*, 213. 'The only time when one hears people singing', diary entry of 10 June, 1942, *ibid*, 354.

4. FITS AND STARTS

'I first thought of it in 1943', Orwell to Fred Warburg, 22 October 1948, *Complete Works Volume XIX*, 457. The letter to Roger Senhouse was sent on 26 December 1948, *Complete Works Volume XIX*, 487–88. Davison prints and usefully discusses Orwell's notes for 'The Quick and the Dead' and 'The Last Man in Europe' as an appendix to *Complete Works Volume XV*, 356–70.

The 'As I Please' column about totalitarianism's disregard for objective truth appeared in *Tribune* on 4 February 1944, *Complete Works Volume XVI*, 88–9. The review of Hayek's *The Road to Serfdom* appeared in the *Observer* on 9 April 1944, *Complete Works Volume XVI*, 149. For the letter to Noel Willmett, *ibid*, 190–1. On Baker, and Orwell's correspondence with C.D. Darlington, Davison, ed., *The Lost Orwell*, 128–33.

The letter to Rayner Heppenstall was sent on 17 July 1944, *Complete Works Volume XVI*, 290–1. George Woodcock's memory of listening to Orwell's tea-table conversations is in *The Crystal Spirit: A Study of George*

Orwell (1967), 28. Warburg reprints the internal Secker memorandum in *All Authors Are Equal* (1973), 93.

'. . . quite an unpleasant thing to have', Orwell to Anne Popham, 15 March 1946, *Complete Works Volume XVIII*, 153. For the diary entry about 'my island in the Hebrides', *Complete Works Volume XII: A Patriot After All: 1940–1941*, 188. 'Freedom and Happiness' appeared in *Tribune* on 4 January 1946, *Complete Works Volume XVIII*, 13–16. The letter to Warburg about Zamyatin was sent on 22 November 1948, *Complete Works Volume XIX*, 471–2. 'Just Junk—But Who Could Resist It?' appeared in the *London Evening Standard*, 5 January 1946, *Complete Works Volume XVIII*, 17–19.

5. JURA DAYS

The letter to Hugh Slater, whom Orwell addresses by his alternative name of 'Humphrey', was sent on 26 September 1946, *Complete Works Volume XVIII* 408. For Orwell's relationship with David Holbrook, see Taylor, *Orwell: The Life*, 377–79.

'You and the Atom Bomb' appeared in *Tribune* on 19 October 1945, *Complete Works Volume XVII*, 319–21. 'Second Thoughts on James Burnham', *Complete Works Volume XVIII*, 268–284. Introduction to Jack London, *Love of Life and Other Stories*, *Complete Works Volume XVIII*, 351–7. 'The Prevention of Literature' appeared in *Polemic*, January 1946, *Complete Works Volume XVIII*, 369–80. 'Politics and the English Language', *Horizon*, April 1946, *Complete Works Volume XVIII*, 421–30.

The letters sent from Jura in the spring of 1947 which refer to progress on *Nineteen Eighty-Four* were sent, respectively, to Frank D. Barber (15 April), George Woodcock (26 May), and Leonard Moore (21 May). *Complete Works Volume XIX*, 126, 146–7, 144–5. Orwell wrote to Warburg on 31 May, *ibid*, 149–50.

Davison prints the text of 'Such, Such Were the Joys' in *Complete Works Volume XIX*, 356–87. See also his prefatory note.

The letter to Sonia was sent on 12 April 1947, *Complete Works Volume XIX*, 122–4. On Sonia and her possible contribution to *Nineteen Eighty-Four*, see Hilary Spurling, *The Girl from the Fiction Department: A Portrait of Sonia Orwell* (2002), *passim*. The letter to Eleanor Jaques of 19 September 1932 is reproduced in *Complete Works Volume X*, 269. Michael G. Brennan discusses Orwell's attempt to equate religious faith with left- and right-wing forms of autocracy in *George Orwell and Religion* (2017), *passim*. The unpublished review of Laski's *Faith, Reason and Civilisation* is printed in *Complete Works Volume XVI*, 122–5. For 'End of the Century', see Sally Conian, 'Orwell and the Origins of Nineteen Eighty-Four', *Times Literary Supplement*, 31 December 1999.

'My book is getting on very slowly', letter to George Woodcock, 9 June 1947, *Complete Works Volume XIX*, 154–5. 'I am getting on fairly well', letter to Leonard Moore, 28 July 1947, *Complete Works Volume XIX*, 177–8. The letter to Warburg was sent on 1 September, *ibid*, 196–7.

'I have been in wretched health', letter to Arthur Koestler, 20 September 1947, *Complete Works Volume XIX*, 206–7. 'I haven't got on as fast as I should', letter to George Woodcock, 21 October 1947, *ibid*, 221. The letter to Leonard Moore which complains of suffering from 'inflammation of the lungs' was sent on 31 October, *ibid*, 224. A subsequent letter about intending to stay in bed to try to recuperate followed on 7 November, *ibid*, 225. 'I've really been very bad for several months', letter to Koestler, 24 November, *ibid*, 226–7. The letter to Frederick Tomlinson of the *Observer* was sent on the same day, *ibid*, 227.

'I think I am now really getting better', letter to Moore, 30 November 1947, *Complete Works Volume XIX*, 231. Second letter dated 7 December, *ibid*, 233–4. Orwell wrote to Celia Kirwan on the same day, *ibid*, 233. The letter to Julian Symons from Hairmyres is dated 26 December, *ibid*, 236.

'Today when I was X-rayed', letter to Celia Kirwan, 20 January 1948, *Complete Works Volume XIX*, 257. The remark about being 'frightfully weak & thin' was made in a second letter to Celia, dated 27 May, *ibid*, 344. 'I can't do any serious work', letter to Symons, 2 January 1948, *ibid*, 249–50. The progress report to Warburg was sent on 4 February, *ibid*, 264.

The letter to Roger Senhouse is dated 'Thursday' (either 13 or 20 May), *Complete Works Volume XIX*, 337–8. 'Of course I have got to go on living a semi-invalid life', letter to Moore, 15 July 1948, *ibid*, 403. Warburg's letter of 19 July is reproduced in *Complete Works Volume XIX*, 408–9.

'Jura was where Orwell wanted to be', Warburg, *All Authors Are Equal*, 101. 'I only get up for half a day', letter to Moore, 3 August 1948, *Complete Works Volume XIX*, 414. Letter to Astor dated 9 October 1948, *ibid*, 450. Subsequent letters to Symons and Powell dated 29 October and 15 November, *ibid*, 460, 467. Letters to Moore and Warburg dated 22 October, *ibid*, 456–7. On the attempts to procure a typist, letter to Moore dated 29 October 1948 and from Senhouse, 2 November, *ibid*, 459–60 and 463. Warburg discusses the typing of *Nineteen Eighty-Four*'s final draft and the idea that Orwell 'might have killed himself by gross negligence' in *All Authors*, 101–2. Sonia's remarks are quoted by Fyvel in *George Orwell: A Personal Memoir*, 160.

Letter to Warburg of 22 November 1948, *Complete Works Volume XIX*, 471–2. The letter to Gwen O'Shaughnessy is dated 28 November, *ibid*, 475–6. Letter to Moore sent 4 December, *ibid*, 478. Letter to

Tosco Fyvel, 18 December, *ibid*, 484. Avril's letter of 14 December, *ibid*, 482–3. 'The latter I will do & send', letter to David Astor, 21 December, *ibid*, 485–6.

6. THE LAST MAN IN EUROPE

Warburg's report on *Nineteen Eighty-Four*, dated 13 December 1948, is reproduced in *All Authors*, 103–6. Farrer's comments are printed in *Complete Works Volume XIX*, 482. Orwell's letter to Warburg is dated 21 December, *ibid*, 486–7.

'I hope the poor fellow will do well', Bruce Dick to David Astor, 5 January 1949, *Complete Works Volume XX*, 13–14. For Tosco Fyvel and his wife Mary's visit to Cranham, T.R. Fyvel, *George Orwell: A Personal Memoir* (1982), 162. 'I don't think he'll live more than a year', *All Authors*, 109. The letter to Richard Rees about proof-correcting was sent on 28 January, *Complete Works Volume XX*, 28–29.

'I mucked it up really', letter to Dwight Macdonald, 27 January 1949, *Complete Works Volume XX*, 27–28. 'I will send you a copy of my new book', letter to Celia Kirwan, 13 February, *ibid*, 41. The letter to Roger Senhouse was sent on 2 March 1949, *ibid*, 50.

Warburg reprises his letter of 8 March in *All Authors*, 110. 'I feel too lousy', letter to Celia Kirwan, 27 February or 6 March, *Complete Works Volume XX*, 49. The letters to Rees and Robert Giroux were sent, respectively, on 6 April and 14 April, ibid, 81 and 84–5. For the letter to Warburg of 22 April, *ibid*, 95. 'Most deadly ill', letter to S.M. Levitas dated 2 May, *ibid*, 104. 'I've been rather bad', letter to Astor, 9 May 1949, *ibid*, 108. For Warburg's letter of 13 May, *All Authors*, 111.

For the letter of 16 May to Warburg, *Complete Works Volume XX*, 116–17. Morland's report, *ibid*, 122. Orwell's letter to Warburg about his examination, *ibid*, 121–2. For Muggeridge on *Nineteen Eighty-Four*, Taylor, *Orwell: The Life*, 402–3. Most of Warburg's letter of 30 May is reproduced in *All Authors*, 113–14.

Meyers prints a selection of reviews of *Nineteen Eighty-Four* in *George Orwell: The Critical Heritage*. Warburg discusses sales figures in *All Authors*, 114–15. For the reactions of early readers, David Pryce-Jones to author; a summary of John Dos Passos's letter of 8 October 1949 is included in *Complete Works Volume XX*, 174.

Orwell's letter to Warburg of 22 August 1949, *Complete Works Volume XX*, 159. The description of his wedding to Sonia is taken from an unpublished memoir by her friend Janetta Parladé (private collection). For the final weeks, *Orwell: The Life*, 416–18.

7. COLD WAR WARRIORS

For Orwell's letter to Vernon Richards of 22 June 1949, *Complete Works Volume XX*, 140–1. Peregrine Worsthorne, quoted in Frances Stonor

Saunders, *Who Paid the Piper? The CIA and the Cultural Cold War* (1999), 300. Orwell's 'statement' is reproduced and discussed by Davison, *Complete Works Volume XX*, 134–6. Orwell's letter to Moore about Sidney Sheldon's proposal was sent on 22 August, *ibid*, 158–9.

'Found the P.M. absorbed in George Orwell's book 1984', Lord Moran, *Winston Churchill: The Struggle for Survival: 1940-1965* (1966), 19 February 1953. Burgess quotation from *1985*, 18; 'Let's be sensible', *ibid*, 63, 67. For Orwell's specific targeting of the Soviet regime, see Robert Conquest, 'Orwell, Socialism and the Cold War', in Rodden, ed., *Cambridge Companion*, 130.

For the CBS Studio One dramatization of 1953, see David Ryan, *George Orwell on Screen: Adaptations, Documentaries and Docudramas on Film and Television* (2018), 13–21. On Rathvon, Stein, and the CIA's involvement in the 1956 Hollywood adaptation, Ryan, 53–62, and Stonor Saunders, 295–8. Ryan provides an extensive discussion of the 1954 BBC version and summarises press reaction, 22–38.

Kingsley Amis, letter to M.G. Sherlock of 5 April 1969, reproduced in Zachary Leader, ed., *The Letters of Kingsley Amis* (2000), 710–11. Czeslaw Milosz, quoted in Meyers, *George Orwell: The Critical Heritage*, 286. For Fyvel's analysis of press comment, *George Orwell: A Personal Memoir*, 201. Timothy Garton-Ash,

'Orwell For Our Time', *Guardian*, 5 May 2001. Crick writes about differing interpretations of the novel in '*Nineteen Eighty-Four*: context and controversy', Rodden, ed., *Cambridge Companion*, 146. For British parliamentary proposals subjected to 'the Orwell test', David Dwan, *Liberty, Equality & Humbug*, 1.

David Ryan supplies useful details of the 1965 BBC version in *George Orwell on Screen*, 88–93. Gordon Phelps, 'The Novel Today' in Boris Ford, ed., *The Pelican Guide to English Literature Volume 7: The Modern Age* (1961), 492. Woodcock, *The Crystal Spirit*, 49. Raymond Williams writes about *Nineteen Eighty-Four* in his Fontana Modern Masters study *Orwell* (1971), 74–80.

8. NEARING THE SELL-BY DATE

Christopher Small, *The Road to Miniluv: George Orwell, the State and God* (1975), 13. On the UK political scene in the 1970s, Phillip Whitehead, ed., *The Writing on the Wall: Britain in the Seventies* (1985), *passim*. For an account of the 1980 Olympic Games and their Orwellian resonances, see

Christopher Booker, *The Games War* (1980), *passim*.

On Sonia's contract with Marvin Rosenblum, see Ryan, *George Orwell on Screen*, 141. For Michael Radford's film, and the 1984 Apple ad, *ibid*, 135–156 and 221–2. Ian Macdonald writes about Love and Spirit in *The People's Music* (2003), 117–22 and 163. Hugh Hopper, quoted in Graham Bennett, *Soft Machine: Out-Bloody-Rageous* (205), 246. The lyrics to 'Tales from the Riverbank' are reproduced in Paul Weller, *Suburban 100: Selected Lyrics* (2007), 17–18.

9. THE POST-TRUTH WORLD

Christopher Hitchens, *Orwell's Victory*, 52–4. On Burma in the late 1990s, see Emma Larkin, *Secret Histories: Finding George Orwell in a Burmese Teashop* (2005). Ron Suskind, quoted in Owen Bennett-Jones, 'Trouble at the BBC', *London Review of Books*, 20 December 2018, 32. Michael Brennan draws attention to the significance of the date 4 April in *George Orwell and Religion*, 147. Woodcock writes about *Nineteen Eighty-Four*'s 'cathartic' effect on Orwell in *The Crystal Spirit*, 55.

CHRONOLOGY

25 June 1903. Eric Arthur Blair born to Richard Walmesley Blair and his wife, Ida, in Motihari, Bengal.

1904. Ida Blair returns to England with Eric and her daughter Marjorie. A second daughter, Avril, is born in 1908. The family settles at Henley-on-Thames, Oxfordshire.

20 May 1910. Death of King Edward VII and accession of George V.

1911–1916. Boarder at St Cyprian's, a preparatory school at Eastbourne, Sussex.

28 July 1914. Beginning of First World War.

8 March 1917. Start of Russian Revolution.

1917–1921. King's Scholar at Eton College, Berkshire.

11 November 1918. End of First World War.

1922–1927. Serves in the Indian Imperial Police in Burma. Resigns while on leave in England in the autumn of 1927.

January 1924. First Labour government takes office in UK.

3 May 1926. UK General Strike.

1927–1932. Variously engaged in tramping excursions in the English Home Counties, staying with his parents in Southwold, Suffolk, living in a working-class district of Paris, and school-teaching. In November 1932 decides to change his name to 'George Orwell'.

24–29 October 1929. Wall Street Crash.

19 September 1931. UK goes off the Gold Standard.

27 October 1931. Landslide General Election victory for Ramsay Mac-Donald's National Government.

9 January 1933. Publishes his first book, *Down and Out in Paris and London*. While teaching at Fray's College, Uxbridge, Middlesex, is taken seriously ill with pneumonia. Returns to Southwold to recuperate.

30 January 1933. Hitler becomes Chancellor of Germany.

4 March 1933. Franklin D. Roosevelt becomes US President.

October 1934. Publishes first novel, *Burmese Days*.

November 1934. Moves to London to work part-time in a Hampstead bookshop.

11 March 1935. Publishes second novel, *A Clergyman's Daughter*.

January to March 1936. Travels in the north of England to collect material for a book on the depressed areas.

20 January 1936. Death of King George V and accession of Edward VIII.

7 March 1936. Germany reoccupies the Rhineland.

April 1936. Moves to The Stores, Wallington, Hertfordshire.

20 April 1936. Publication of third novel, *Keep the Aspidistra Flying*.

9 June 1936. Marries Eileen O'Shaughnessy.

18 July 1936. Spanish Civil War begins.

10 December 1936. Edward VIII abdicates and is succeeded by George VI.

December 1936. Leaves for Spain to fight on the Republican side in the Spanish Civil War.

January to June 1937. Serves in Independent Labour Party contingent with the POUM militia on the Aragon Front.

8 March 1937. Publishes *The Road to Wigan Pier*. In July returns to Wallington.

20 May 1937. Shot through the throat by Fascist sniper, but narrowly survives.

March to September 1938. Patient at Preston Hall sanatorium, Kent. Leaves for French Morocco to convalesce.

25 April 1938. Publication of *Homage to Catalonia*. Seriously ill with tubercular lesion in one lung.

April 1939. Returns to Wallington.

12 June 1939. Publication of fourth novel, *Coming Up for Air*.

1 September 1939. Second World War begins.

11 March 1940. Publishes *Inside the Whale and Other Essays*.

May 1940. Moves to Regent's Park, London. Joins Local Defence Volunteers (the Home Guard).

10 May 1940. German armies break across the borders of three neutral states, Belgium, Holland, and Luxembourg, and invade France. Winston Churchill succeeds Neville Chamberlain as UK Prime Minister.

14 June 1940. Paris occupied by German army.

7 September 1940. Start of *Luftwaffe* bombing raids on London ('the Blitz').

19 February 1941. Publishes *The Lion and the Unicorn: Socialism and the English Genius*.

April 1941. Moves to St John's Wood, London.

22 June 1941. Germany invades Soviet Union.

August 1941. Takes up appointment as Talks Assistant, subsequently Talks Producer, in the Indian section of the BBC's Eastern Service.

7 December 1941. Japanese attack US Naval Base at Pearl Harbor. America enters the war.

Summer 1942. Moves to Maida Vale, London.

November 1943. Leaves BBC to take up the post of Literary Editor of *Tribune*. Leaves Home Guard on medical grounds. Begins work on *Animal Farm*.

28 November–1 December 1943. Tehran Conference, at which the 'Big Three' (Roosevelt, Stalin, and

February 1944. Completes *Animal Farm*.

Summer 1944. Makes first visit to Jura, Inner Hebrides.

June 1944. He and Eileen adopt a son, Richard Horatio Blair.

October 1944. Moves to Canonbury Square, Islington, London.

February to March 1945. War correspondent for the *Observer* and the *Manchester Evening News* in France and Germany.

29 March 1945. Death of Eileen Blair.

17 August 1945. Publishes fifth novel, *Animal Farm*.

September 1945. Pays second visit to Jura.

October 1945. Writes essay 'You

Churchill) determine the shape of the post-war world.

6 June 1944. Allied invasion of Occupied Europe begins with assault on Normandy beaches.

12 April 1945. Roosevelt dies and is succeeded by Harry S. Truman.

30 April 1945. Death of Hitler.

7 May 1945. End of war in Europe.

26 July 1945. After winning UK General Election, the Labour Party's Clement Attlee succeeds Churchill as UK Prime Minister.

6 and 9 August 1945. First atomic bombs dropped on Japanese cities of Hiroshima and Nagasaki.

1 September 1945. Second World War ends. 'Free elections' in Poland, Rumania, and Bulgaria followed by the installation of pro-Soviet satellite governments.

and the Atom Bomb' for *Tribune*, which includes first use of the phrase 'Cold War'.

February 1946. Publishes *Critical Essays*.

5 March 1946. Churchill, in a speech at Westminster College, Fulton, Missouri, coins the phrase 'Iron Curtain' to describe the division of Western democracies and the Soviet-dominated regimes of Eastern Europe.

May to October 1946. Living at Barnhill, Jura. At work on *Nineteen Eighty-Four*.

1 July 1946. The US begins a programme of nuclear testing at its base on Bikini Atoll in the Marshall Islands.

Mid-October 1946. Returns to Canonbury Square.

19 December 1946. Beginning of the First Indochina War.

April 1947. Returns to Jura.

May 1947. Sends his publisher a version of 'Such, Such Were the Joys'.

5 June 1947. US Secretary of State George Marshall lays out a plan to rebuild Western Europe.

August 1947. Publishes *The English People* in the series *Britain in Pictures*.

November 1947. Finishes first draft of *Nineteen Eighty-Four*.

December 1947. Admitted to Hairmyres Hospital, East Kilbride, Scotland, with tuberculosis of left lung.

January to July 1948. Remains at Hairmyres.

3 April 1948. Truman signs the Economic Recovery Act, intended to restore the infrastructure of post-war Europe.

24 June 1948. Stalin orders the Berlin Blockade.

Early November 1948. Finishes *Nineteen Eighty-Four*. Final version sent to agent and publisher a month later. Now gravely ill.

2 November 1948. Truman defeats the Republican candidate Thomas Dewey in the US presidential election.

January 1949. Leaves Jura for the last time for Cotswold Sanatorium, Cranham, Gloucestershire.

8 June 1949. UK publication of his final novel, *Nineteen Eighty-Four*.

13 June 1949. US publication of *Nineteen Eighty-Four*.

Early September 1949. Transferred to University College Hospital, London.

1 October 1949. Mao Zedong declares the foundation of the People's Republic of China.

13 October 1949. Marries Sonia Brownell.

21 January 1950. Dies of pulmonary tuberculosis, aged 46.

26 January 1950. Buried at All Saints, Sutton Courtenay, Berkshire.

INDEX

afterlife, 39
alternative facts, 165–67
alternative reality, 39, 164–67
American Committee for Cultural
  Freedom (ACCF), 129–30
Amis, Kingsley, 134–35, 147, 148–49
Apple Macintosh, 152
Assignment in Utopia (Lyons), 41
Astor, David, 63, 113, 114
atomic bomb, 68
Attlee, Clement, 117

Baker, John R., 56–58
Barcelona, 35–38
BBC, 45–47
Blair, Avril, 10, 66, 85, 96, 104, 114
Blair, Ida, 10
Blair, Marjorie, 10
Blair, Richard Horatio, 60–61, 66, 84,
  85, 114
Blair, Richard Walmesley, 9–10
boat accident, 84–85
Booker, Christopher, 149
Book of the Month Club, 103–4, 110
Bowie, David, 154–55
Bracken, Brendan, 45
Bramah, Ernest, 42
Brave New World (Huxley), 42–43, 64
Brazil, 160
Brexit, 162–63
Brown, Jerry, 156
Brownell, Sonia, 8, 76–82, 95, 113,
  114, 150, 169

Buddicom, Jacintha, 13
Bukharin, Nikolai, 40–41
Bumstead, Jack, 16
Burgess, Anthony, 15, 124–25, 126,
  146, 147–48
Burma, 161
Burma Imperial Police, 11–13
Burnham, James, 68–69

California, Randy, 153
'California Über Alles' (Dead
  Kennedys), 156
Cartier, Rudolph, 132
Chernobyl disaster, 137
Christen, Miranda, 75
Churchill, Winston, 124
CIA Office of Policy Coordination,
  128–29
class, Orwell's obsession with,
  10–11
Cold War, 5–7, 127–28, 142
Collapse of Democracy, The (Moss),
  147
Colls, Robert, 32
Communism, 27, 110, 119, 135–36,
  144
Connolly, Cyril, 11, 14, 72
Conquest, Robert, 127
Constantine, Murray, 41
Conway, Kellyanne, 165
Corryvreckan whirlpool, 85
Cranham, 96, 101, 106, 112
Crick, Bernard, 5, 137

Cronkite, Walter, 149–50
'Cygnet Committee' (Bowie), 154–55

Dakin, Henry, 85
Dakin, Jane, 85
Dakin, Lucy, 85
Darlington, Cyril, 57
Davison, Peter, 123, 125
Dead Kennedys, 156
Deakins, Roger, 151
Democratic People's Republic of
    Korea, 158–59, 161, 162
Dick, Bruce, 101
Dickens, Charles, 124
Dos Passos, John, 38, 111
doublethink, 80–81, 127
Dwan, David, 137–38
dystopian literature, Orwell's interest
    in, 41–43

Eastern Europe, *Nineteen Eighty-
    Four*'s impact in, 135–37. *See
    also* Soviet Union
Empson, William, 46
Eurythmics, 152–53

Fabian Society, 134
Facecrime, 127
failure, Orwell's obsession with, 14–15
Faith, Reason, and Civilisation
    (Laski), 81
Fane, Julian, 147
Farrar, David, 99
Fascism, 24–27, 37–38, 110, 119,
    163–64, 166
financial crisis of autumn 1931, 31
Fletcher, Robin, 87–88
Fyvel, Tosco, 101, 136

Garton-Ash, Timothy, 137
Gilliam, Terry, 160
Giroux, Robert, 102

Glengarrisdale, 85
golden country, 22–23
Gollancz, Victor, 31, 33, 39–40, 59,
    71–72

Hairmyres, 87–91
Hayek, F.A., 54
Hitchens, Christopher, 136, 158–59
Hitler, Adolf, 24–27, 28, 155
Holbrook, David, 67
Hopper, Hugh, 154
Hurt, John, 151
Huxley, Aldous, 32, 42–43, 64, 141

immortality, 39
Iron Heel, The (London), 42, 43, 69, 98

Jam, the, 156–57
Jaques, Eleanor, 79
Jenkin, Sir Bernard, 163
Jonathan Cape publishing house, 59
Junior Spies, 127
Jura, 62–63, 66, 71, 76–77, 82–87,
    91–96

Keller, Hans, 146
Kennard, Michael, 104
Kim Jong Il, 158–59
Kirwan, Celia, 86–87, 89–90
Kneale, Nigel, 132
Koestler, Arthur, 56, 85, 86
Kopp, Georges, 38

Larkin, Emma, 161
Laski, Harold, 81
Left Book Club, 31, 33
Life, 117, 119
London, Jack, 42, 43, 69, 98
Love, 153
Luce, Henry, 117, 119
Lyons, Eugene, 41
Lysenko, Trofim Denisovich, 56–57

MacDonald, Ramsay, 30, 31
Managerial Revolution, The
    (Burnham), 68–69
manipulation, as key theme in
    Orwell's early work, 18–20
Marshall Plan, 6
McCarthy, Joseph, 128
Milosz, Czeslaw, 135–36
Moore, Leonard, 94
Moran, Lord, 124
Morland, Andrew, 105–7, 112
Moss, Robert, 147
Muggeridge, Malcolm, 8, 35, 43, 101,
    107, 113
music, inspired by *Nineteen Eighty-
    Four*, 152–57

National Industrial Recovery Act,
    117–18
nature, Orwell's love of, 22–23
Nelson, Bill, 154
Nevinson, C.R.W., 140
New Deal, 117–18
Newspeak, 121, 143, 148
Nickell, Paul, 128
Nicolson, Harold, 1
1985 (Burgess), 126, 146, 147–48
'1984' (Spirit), 153
1984 Revisited, 149–50
Nineteen Eighty-Four
    advance copies of, 104–5
    as Cold War weapon, 127–28
    completion of, 70–72, 93–97
    connections between Thirties
        quartet and, 17–27
    contemporary relevance of, 162–67
    cover art of, 139–40
    critical reception of, 1–2, 109–10
    critical reinterpretation of, 140–44,
        145
    draft of, 67, 89
    familiar landscape of, 6–7

historical context of, 5–6, 110–11,
    167–68
hope in, 121–23
impact of, 111, 123–26, 133–39,
    161–62
influences on, 41–48, 51–52, 63–65
intended message of, 159–60
manuscript of, 169–70
misinformation regarding, 117–21
novels inspired by, 126, 146–49
obstacles to writing of, 58–63,
    66–68, 84–91
Orwell's life experiences in, 15–17
parallels between life in North
    Korea and, 158–59
parallels between Orwell's Jura
    diary and, 82–84
planning for, 52–58, 62–65, 67–70
pop music inspired by, 152–57
popular reaction to, 4–5, 6–7, 107
profit from, 104, 108, 110
progress on, 84
publication of, 100–104, 107–8
publisher's reception of, 98–100
screen adaptations of, 128–33,
    138–39, 150–53, 160
similarities between 'Such, Such
    Were the Joys' and, 73–76
Sonia Brownell's influence on,
    77–82
success of, 7, 108–12, 123, 127, 133,
    141, 160
synopsis of, 2–4
versatility of, 137–39, 160–61
working-class English life in, 34
North Korea, 158–59, 161, 162

Olympic Games (1984), 149
Orwell, George
    adolescence of, 11–12
    ambitions in youth, 28
    chronology of life of, 181–87

Orwell, George (cont.)
   and completion of *Nineteen Eighty-
      Four*, 70–72, 93–97, 167–68
   on critical reception of *Nineteen
      Eighty-Four*, 2
   early years of, 9–11, 72–76
   employment with BBC's Eastern
      Service, 45–47
   employment with Burma Imperial
      Police, 11–13
   experiences of, in *Nineteen Eighty-
      Four*, 15–17
   fatalism of, 94–95, 100
   fights in Spanish Civil War, 34–40
   final months of, 91–97
   and hope in *Nineteen Eighty-Four*,
      121–23
   illness and death of, 7–8, 113–14
   illness following boat accident,
      84–85
   illness following Spanish Civil
      War, 40
   illness with tuberculosis, 62, 85–87,
      91–96, 99, 102–4
   and impact of *Nineteen Eighty-
      Four*, 124–26
   impetus for works of, 51–52, 54
   interest and involvement in politics,
      30–32
   interest in dystopian literature,
      41–43
   Jura diary of, 82–84, 92, 97
   love of nature and women, 22–23
   manipulation in early work of,
      18–20
   marriage to Eileen, 33–34
   marriage to Sonia, 113
   and misinformation regarding
      Nineteen Eighty-Four, 117–20
   name of, 14
   obsession with class and social
      status, 10–11
   obsession with rats, 16–17
   obsession with totalitarian mind,
      40–41, 43–44
   and obstacles to *Nineteen Eighty-
      Four*, 58–63, 66–68, 84–91
   outsider status of, 13–15
   and planning for *Nineteen Eighty-
      Four*, 52–58, 62–65, 67–70
   political beliefs in early work,
      28–30
   and publication of *Nineteen Eighty-
      Four*, 100–104
   receives advance copy of *Nineteen
      Eighty-Four*, 104–5
   returns to London, 45
   self-criticism of, 102
   success of, 14–15
   and success of *Nineteen Eighty-
      Four*, 112
   travels to north of England,
      31–33
   treated for tuberculosis, 87–91,
      100–101, 105–8
   works
     see also *Nineteen Eighty-Four*
     Animal Farm, 51, 58–60, 129,
      131
     'As I Please' column, 54
     'Boys' Weeklies', 14
     Burmese Days, 12, 18, 19, 20–23,
      28–29
     A Clergyman's Daughter, 18–19,
      20–22, 29–30, 58, 102
     Coming Up for Air, 18, 19–22,
      23–27
     *Down and Out in Paris and
      London*, 13–14, 17
     full-length novels, 17–18
     Homage to Catalonia, 14, 40, 59
     'Inside the Whale', 43
     'Just Junk—But Who Could
      Resist It?', 65

Keep the Aspidistra Flying, 18, 19, 20–22, 23, 29–30, 51, 102
'The Last Man in Europe', 52, 54
The Lion and the Unicorn: Socialism and the English Genius, 44, 59, 123
'Looking Back on the Spanish War', 38–39, 40
'Politics and the English Language', 70
'The Prevention of Literature', 69–70
'The Quick and the Dead', 52
The Road to Wigan Pier, 14, 31, 34
'A Smoking-room Story', 112
'Such, Such Were the Joys', 72–76
'You and the Atom Bomb', 68
'Orwellian', 125, 162–63
O'Shaughnessy, Eileen, 33–34, 38, 60–61, 81
O'Shaughnessy, Gwen, 96, 104

Patriot Act, 138
PEN conference, 55–56, 57
Phelps, Gilbert, 142
Phillips, Anthony, 154
politics
    see also Communism; Fascism; socialism; totalitarianism
    and contemporary relevance of *Nineteen Eighty-Four*, 162–67
    in Orwell's early work, 28–30
    Orwell's interest and involvement with, 30–32
    and Spanish Civil War, 34–40
    in Thirties quartet, 23–27
Pollitt, Harry, 36
pop music, inspired by *Nineteen Eighty-Four*, 152–57
Powell, Anthony, 8, 9, 13, 63, 101, 114
Pritchett, V.S., 109

Pryce-Jones, David, 111
Psychological Warfare Workshop (PWW), 128–29

Radford, Michael, 150, 151, 160
Rahv, Philip, 1
Rathvon, Peter, 129, 130
rats, Orwell's obsession with, 16–17
Read, Herbert, 141
reality, alternative, 39, 164–67
Red Scare, 128
'Red Telephone, The' (Love), 153
Rees, Richard, 13, 89, 97, 102, 104
'Revolt into Style' (Nelson), 154
Revolution Island (Fane), 147
Road to Serfdom, The (Hayek), 54
Roberts, William, 140
Roosevelt, Franklin D., 117–18
Rosenblum, Marvin, 150
Russian Hide and Seek (Amis), 147, 148–49
Ryan, David, 128
Rykoff, Alexei, 40–41

Sakeld, Brenda, 79
Sanders, Bernie, 138
Science and the Planned State (Baker), 56–57
scientific freedom, 56–57
Secker, Martin, 59
Secker & Warburg, 59, 64, 103
second-hand shops, 65
Secret of the League, The (Bramah), 42
Senhouse, Roger, 51, 90, 94
'Sexcrime' (Eurythmics), 152–53
Sheldon, Sidney, 119–20
Siegel, Daniel G., 169
Sillen, Samuel, 2
Small, Christopher, 145
socialism, 32, 44, 54, 81, 98, 118–19, 120
Socialism and the Intellectuals, 134

Sokal Hoax, 161–62
Soul of the Soulless City, The
    (Nevinson), 140
Soviet show trials, 40–41
Soviet Union, 56–58, 63–64, 81,
    127–28, 137
Spanish Civil War, 34–40
Spicer, Sean, 164, 165
Spirit, 153
Spurling, Hilary, 77–78, 80, 81
Stalin, Joseph, 5, 24–27, 28
'Standards' (Jam), 156
Stein, Sol, 129, 130, 131
St Syprian's, 11–12, 72–75
Suskind, Ron, 164
Swastika Night (Constantine), 41
Symons, Julian, 2, 109

'Tales from the Riverbank' (Jam), 156
Tehran Conference (1943), 51–52, 54
Thatcher, Margaret, 149
Thirties, The (Muggeridge), 43
totalitarianism, 24–27, 38–41, 43–44,
    69–70, 110, 118–19, 127
Trilling, Diana, 1
Truman, Harry S., 6
Trump, Donald, 163–66
truth, loss of objective, 39, 164–67
tuberculosis, 62, 85–95, 99, 100–108

United Automobile Workers Union
    (UAW), 118–19
United Workers Marxist Party
    (POUM), 36–37

Wakeman, Rick, 154
Warburg, Fred
  on misinformation regarding
    Nineteen Eighty-Four, 118–19,
    120

on Orwell's ability to work, 112
on Orwell's early career, 14
on Orwell's final months, 95
and Orwell's medical treatment,
    105–7
and publication of *Animal
    Farm*, 59
and publication of *Nineteen
    Eighty-Four*, 90–91, 103
reaction to *Nineteen Eighty-Four*,
    98–100
on success of *Nineteen Eighty-Four*,
    105
Warburg, Pamela, 101
war crimes, 44–45
Watson, Peter, 14
Watson, Susan, 62, 66, 67
Waugh, Evelyn, 13
We (Zamyatin), 63–65
Wedgwood, Veronica, 109
Weller, Paul, 156–57
Wells, H.G., 42, 99
West, Rebecca, 109
When the Sleeper Wakes (Wells), 42
Who Says It Can Never Happen Here,
    146
Wilkes, 'Flip', 73–74
Wilkes, 'Sambo', 73–74
Williams, Raymond, 143–44, 145
Willmett, Noel, 55
'Winter of Discontent' of 1978–9,
    146
women, Orwell's love of, 22
Woodcock, George, 61, 71, 84, 142,
    168
Worsthorne, Peregrine, 118

Yagoda, Genrikh, 40–41

Zamyatin, Yevgeny, 63–65